Key stage 3 Oxford history study units

Imperial China

CAROL GLEISNER

Contents

Chapter one
一 **What was China like?**   3

Chapter two
二 **Was China a peaceful country?**   8

Chapter three
三 **What ideas were important in China?**   14

Chapter four
四 **What did the Chinese invent and create?**   23

Chapter five
五 **How did the people live?**   30

Chapter six
六 **How important was trade?**   41

心 Index   48

Preface

OXFORD
UNIVERSITY PRESS

Great Clarendon Street, Oxford OX2 6DP

Oxford University Press is a department of the University of Oxford. It furthers the University's objective of excellence in research, scholarship, and education by publishing worldwide in

Oxford New York

Auckland Cape Town Dar es Salaam
Hong Kong Karachi Kuala Lumpur Madrid
Melbourne Mexico City Nairobi
New Delhi Shanghai Taipei Toronto

With offices in

Argentina Austria Brazil Chile Czech Republic France Greece Guatemala Hungary Italy Japan Poland Portugal Singapore South Korea Switzerland Thailand Turkey Ukraine Vietnam

Oxford is a registered trade mark of Oxford University Press in the UK and in certain other countries

© Oxford University Press 1993

The moral rights of the author have been asserted

Database right Oxford University Press (maker)

First published 1993

10 9 8

All rights reserved. No part of this publication may be reproduced, stored in a retrieval system, or transmitted, in any form or by any means, without the prior permission in writing of Oxford University Press, or as expressly permitted by law, or under terms agreed with the appropriate reprographics rights organization. Enquiries concerning reproduction outside the scope of the above should be sent to the Rights Department, Oxford University Press, at the address above.

You must not circulate this book in any other binding or cover and you must impose this same condition on any acquirer.

ISBN-13: 978-0-19-917193-4
ISBN-10: 0-19-917193-9

Typeset by MS Filmsetting Limited, Frome, Somerset

Printed in China

Preface

This book investigates the history of China from the establishment of the Qin dynasty in 221 BC to the Mongol invasion of AD 1279. It focuses on the key question: '*Was China a great civilisation?*' It begins by looking at some of the credulous comments about China by Marco Polo in the 1290s, and pupils can use these as a reference point - a European perspective on an isolated China - and this gives them the opportunity to look back over time in their assessment. The book invites pupils to suggest possible solutions to 'What makes a civilisation?' In this way, from the start, the application and analysis of an important, relevant and accessible concept is established. Having obtained a hypothesis to this central question, the book poses six sub questions, each reflecting one idea about 'civilisation', to test this in the light of the evidence for China from 221 BC to 1279 AD.

These six sub questions are:
- What was China like?
- Was China a peaceful country?
- What ideas were important in China?
- What did the Chinese invent and create?
- How did the people live?
- How important was trade?

These follow a broad chronological framework, though each question can be studied separately form the others, or they can be studied in a different sequence. At times the pupils are asked to look back to Marco Polo's comments as a benchmark for assessing the hypothesis, and also for change and continuity. The conclusion of the book, and thus of the central question, brings the pupils full circle, back to Marco Polo and other European travellers amazed at what they find and, therefore, the book possesses an entity for study.

The other main focus of the book is to establish the marked differences and outstanding achievements of a self-contained and isolated China during these years, and to emphasise for the pupils both the advanced nature of many of China's inventions, ideas and attitudes in compartison with a contemporary Europe, whilst illustrating the static or less developed nature of other aspects of life in China. This emphasis reflects the concentration on understanding the ideas and attitudes of people in the past. All these issues add to the discussion of 'What makes a civilisation?' and 'Was China a great civilisation during these years?', and create a genuine challenge and historical debate.

Notes to teachers

This book is ideally suited to the fifth area of study in the revised National Curriculum: a world study before 1900.

What was China like?

In 1275 a 17-year-old Italian, Marco Polo, went to China. He travelled with his father and uncle. They all came from Venice, and they stayed in China for 17 years, until 1292. They were not the first Europeans to visit China, but the story that Marco Polo told on his return to Italy seemed so fantastic, that many did not believe it, and laughed.

Here are some of the things he described in Hangzhou, the capital city of China, or 'Heavenly City' as Marco Polo called it:

'There are immense quantities of every kind of food, such as deer, stags, hares, rabbits; and partridges, quails, chickens, and more ducks and geese than one could ever tell. Every day an immense quantity of fish is brought from the Ocean, to a distance of 40 kilometres upstream. One would never think that it could all be sold, yet in a few hours it is all gone, so great is the number of people used to living luxuriously, eating both fish and meat at the same meal. The city has 12,000 bridges, most of which are of stone, and those that cross the main canals and the Great Street are arched up so high, and are so cunningly built, that a large boat can pass beneath them without lowering its masts; yet carts and horses cross them, so well have the streets been kept level. There are numerous cold baths, staffed by attendants of both sexes, who bathe the men and women who go there, for they are used from childhood to washing themselves with cold water at all seasons.'

He also commented on the people of China.

'The natives of Hangzhou are men of peace. They have no skill in handling weapons and do not keep any in their houses. They dislike strife or any sort of disagreement. They pursue their trades and handicrafts with honesty. They love one another so devotedly that a whole district might seem, from the friendly and neighbourly spirit to be a single household. The young ladies are modest, and do not keep watch at the windows gazing at passers-by. The people are superior in their customs and depth of learning, for they are ever intent upon their studies and scientific pursuits. They speak well and clearly, and they greet you courteously.'

Chapter one

This is a picture of Marco Polo. Here is some further information about him:
- He visited China at the end of the period that you are going to investigate.
- China was conquered by the Mongols in AD 1279.
- Marco Polo was liked by the Mongol Emperor, Kublai Khan, who employed him along with other Europeans to help him rule China.
- Marco Polo did not learn Chinese.
- He travelled in many parts of China, and for three years was governor of a Chinese city.
- Marco Polo said that he told only one-half of what he had seen.

EVIDENCE: MARCO POLO

1. List the main points described by Marco Polo.
2. Write a description of China in the 1290s based on these extracts.
3. Which things would contemporary Europeans have found difficult to believe? Give reasons for your answer.
4. Marco Polo said a lot about China, but there were also many amazing things that he omitted. This has caused some historians to doubt his account. How can we find out if his story, even with gaps of information, was accurate or not?
5. How useful is Marco Polo's evidence for an insight into Chinese life?

Chapter one

Was China a great civilisation?

Marco Polo was not the only person to be impressed by China.

'The Chinese have the oldest continuous civilisation in the world — going back some four thousand years — and also the oldest centralised state, which has survived, with interruptions, since 221 BC.'

This was written by a modern historian, A. Clayre, and at the front of his book, *The Heart of the Dragon*, he said that he hoped that it would, *'... make Chinese civilisation — the only surviving civilisation to have grown up and flourished until recently in independence of the West — better understood among some of the three-quarters of the people in the world who are not Chinese.'*

What did he mean by the word civilisation? You are going to investigate this word and attempt a definition. This will then become a framework for your study of China from 221 BC to AD 1279.

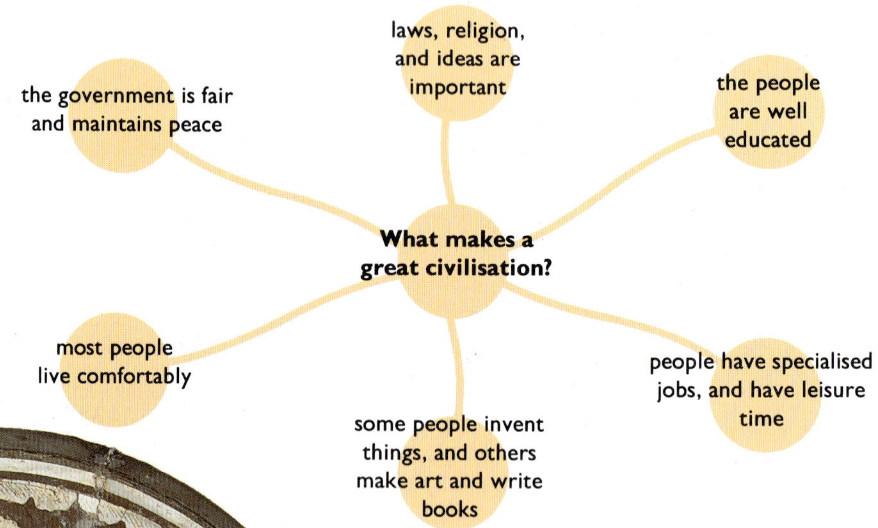

What makes a great civilisation?
- the government is fair and maintains peace
- laws, religion, and ideas are important
- the people are well educated
- people have specialised jobs, and have leisure time
- some people invent things, and others make art and write books
- most people live comfortably

A bronze mirror with mother of pearl inlay from the Tang Dynasty (AD 618–906)

Some more evidence on China

Francis Bacon, a sixteenth-century historian and English politician, said that three inventions — paper with printing, gunpowder, and the magnetic compass — completely changed the Europe of the Middle Ages into the modern world. He died not knowing that these three inventions had been in use in China for a very long time.

Source A
The roof of the palace itself is very high. The walls of the halls and chambers inside are all covered with gold and silver and decorated with pictures of dragons, birds, horsemen, various beasts and battle scenes. The ceiling is similarly decorated. The hall is so vast and wide that a meal might be served here for more than 6000 men.

(Marco Polo describing the Winter Palace in Beijing)

Source B
This is how they worshipped their gods. Each man keeps at home on one of the walls of his room, a statue representing the Supreme God of the Heavens. They burn incense daily, raise their hands and gnash their teeth three times, praying to the god to grant them good understanding and a long, happy, and joyful life. On the floor they have another statue who is god of the things of the earth, to whom they pray for earthly things like fair weather, for the fruits of the earth, for children, and so on.

(Marco Polo on religion in Hangzhou)

Source C
They write with a brush such as painters paint with and make in one figure the several letters containing a single word.

(Friar John describing writing when he visited China from France in 1253)

What was China like?

A ceramic model of an armoured man on horseback from the Tang Dynasty. Note the stirrups, which were a Chinese invention in the third century.

PEOPLE IN THE PAST: WAS CHINA A CIVILISATION?

1. Discuss the diagram opposite. Do you want to add other things to it? You might find it useful to think of other past societies that you have studied when younger, like the Greeks or Egyptians.
2. Study pages 3 to 7, and then copy and fill in the chart below with evidence.
3. Do the Romans seem to be a civilisation? Explain your answer.
4. Do the Anglo-Saxons seem to be a civilisation? Explain your answer.
5. Look at Marco Polo's comments again on page 3, and the evidence about China on pages 4 and 5. Do you think China was a civilisation? What answer do you have? Yes it was. No it was not. I'm not sure. Explain your answer.

	China	Romans	Anglo-Saxons
laws			
leisure			
comfort			
peace			
education			
others?			

Chapter one

Some evidence on the Romans

Source D
Rome was by far the greatest city of the ancient world. Hundreds of thousands of people lived there. Such a dense population was only made possible by the excellent water supply. Several aqueducts carried water from surrounding hillsides into the city, where it fed public taps and fountains or was piped directly into the homes of the rich.

(R. J. Cootes and L. E. Snellgrove in *The Ancient World*, 1970)

Source E
It was said that the Romans loved 'bread and circuses' because they were happy if they had enough food and something like a circus to amuse them. Their circuses, which were horse and chariot races, took place in special buildings, such as the Circus Maximus in Rome, and the entertainments went on for days. Thousands of slaves and animals were killed during those cruel Roman holidays. In amphitheatres, such as the Colosseum in Rome, gladiators fought their battle of life and death with savage fury.

(R. Pitcher and A. Harris in *Man Makes His Way*, 1969)

A stone carving of a Roman school. Note the slave with a pupil's satchel.

Some evidence on the Anglo-Saxons

Source F
A man could be hanged or beheaded for such crimes as the theft of cattle or goods, fire-raising, or treachery to the king. More often he was whipped or had an arm or foot cut off. The Saxons seem to have felt that there was usually some doubt about a man's guilt except when he was caught red-handed, so they often spared a criminal's life.

(V. Chancellor in *Medieval and Tudor Britain*, 1967)

Source G
Poetry shows that the Anglo-Saxons were alive to the beauty of metalwork and to the impressive splendour of the warrior in grey steel mail, his sword-hilt adorned with gold, his boar-crested helmet and polished spear-tip glancing in the sun. Remains show that skilled weapon smiths and jewellers existed even in the heathen age, and some of their products, such as their garnet-inlaid brooches and buckles, arouse general admiration.

(D. Whitelock in *The Beginnings of English Society*, 1952)

What was China like?

In this illustration Saxon women wind and weave wool, with scenes of hell beneath them

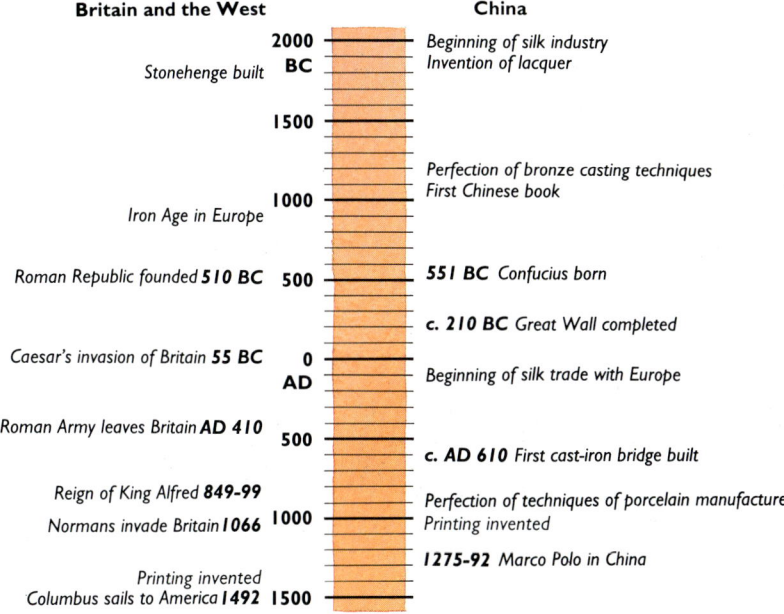

Timeline comparing China and the West

Here is a timeline of the period that you will be studying about China. It covers 3500 years, and makes some comparisons with Europe and Britain. Does this help you make any further conclusions about China as a civilisation?

Summary: Was China a great civilisation?

What answer do you have so far – yes/no/I'm not sure?

In the rest of the book you are going to look closely at this key question. Write a few sentences giving your answer, with reasons, either as an individual or in groups. Put this on paper or as a poster, with today's date, and put it on the classroom wall. At the end of each chapter you will have the chance to develop your ideas further, and add to the display. However, you will find that you need to balance things like peasant hardships and the cruelty of foot-binding for girls and women, with brilliant inventions, beautiful artwork and organised trade.

As you add to and develop these ideas you will be discovering what it was like to live in China during those 1500 years, from 221 BC to AD 1279. You will probably find it exciting, surprising and different from what you now imagine it to be like.

China as a civilisation?

For	Against	Comments

Keeping a chart like this will help you in your investigation and conclusion

Chapter two

Was China a peaceful country?

You need to look at why 221 BC is a significant date for beginning your investigation of China as a civilisation. You also need to learn how China was governed, and whether this resulted in a peaceful country with a united people.

Qin, who became Emperor in 221 BC, was head of a dynasty, which is like being head of a royal family. The Chinese refer to the past in dynasties, just like we might refer to the Dark Ages, the Middle Ages or the Modern Period, spanning several hundred years. Look at the maps and the timeline for the four main dynasties and their dates.

A timeline of the dynasties. Study it carefully. In a paragraph describe the history of China as shown by this timeline. What impression do you get of the country and its rulers from this timeline? The orange areas represent periods of upheaval.

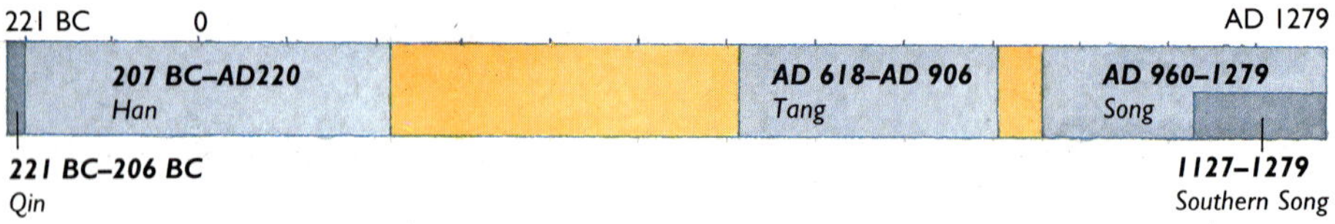

```
221 BC      0                                                              AD 1279
    207 BC–AD220                    AD 618–AD 906      AD 960–1279
    Han                             Tang               Song
221 BC–206 BC                                                    1127–1279
Qin                                                              Southern Song
```

Maps of the four main dynasties. By this time China was 1,800,000 square kilometres, that is almost four times the size of France today. The population was over 60 million.

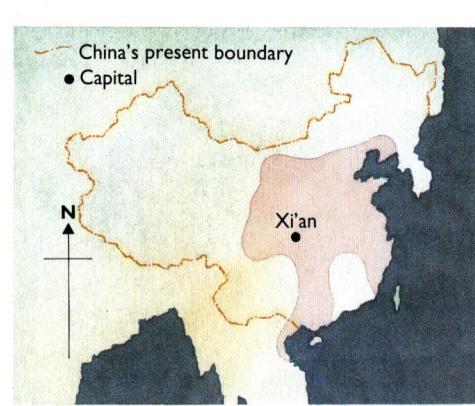
Qin Dynasty

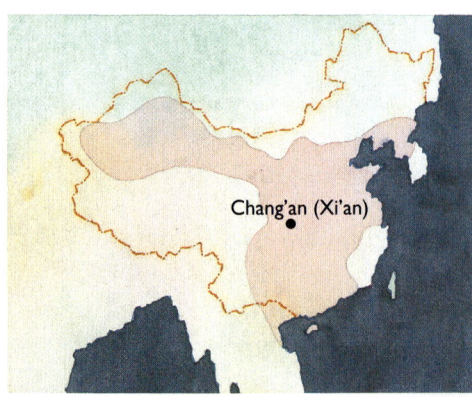
Han Dynasty

Who ruled China from 221 BC?

Even before 221 BC China had a long history. There is prehistoric evidence from 5000 years ago of farming, pottery, religion, money, and of the people being organised under rulers. Bronze items date from 4000 years ago. Even more remarkable is evidence of writing in picture form from just as far back in time. From this early writing the modern Chinese language has evolved.

In 221 BC after a long period of fighting between lords, one with the name of Qin (Chin) became Emperor. From his name we derive the name for China, and from his rule onwards we can recognise a large area of land with common laws, which is one country. There followed many other rulers with differing stories of success and failure, long periods of stability and times of upheaval, until AD 1279 when China was invaded from the North and conquered by the Mongols.

Tang Dynasty

Song Dynasty

CHANGES: THE SIZE OF CHINA

1. Look at the maps. What problems faced any ruler of China?
2. You can see that the capital city changed over time. If present day Europe was one country and was compared to China, it would be like moving the capital from Paris to Rome. What problems would this create?
3. Does the information on this page add anything to your views so far on China as a civilisation? Add your thoughts and ideas to your charts and notes, and keep them as a record.

Qin Shihuangdi: the First Emperor 221-207 BC

What does the word 'Emperor' conjure up in your mind? Just a ruler, or someone very powerful, above all the rest of the people, and beautifully clothed? Or something else?

Qin gave to himself the title 'huangdi' meaning 'great sovereign'. It became the title of all later emperors. As soon as he had proved himself as a great warrior, and taken power, he confiscated every weapon in his new empire and melted them down to be recast as 12 huge bronze statues, weighing over 100,000 kilos each. He believed that his empire would pass to his descendants for 10,000 generations!

He also had axles of carts made to a uniform size. Round copper coins with a square hole in the centre were put into use. Irrigation canals were built as well as the Great Wall, and roads radiated from the capital Xi'an (later known as Chang'an). On the tops of several mountains in his empire Qin Shihuangdi made many inscriptions. Source A shows just a few of them. What do you learn about him from the inscriptions, and from their location?

Penalties were harsh if the laws were broken. Branding, chopping off of hands and of feet, strangulation, and mutilation were some of the punishments. Books were also burned, and scholars were buried alive in a pit (see above). All books, except for those on the history of the Qin period, philosophy, medicine and farming, were destroyed. Execution was ordered for anyone quoting from them.

A peaceful country?

This picture shows Emperor Qin Shihuangdi watching books being burned and scholars being thrown into a pit to be buried alive

Source A
Not until now, when this our emperor
Has made the world one family,
And weapons of warfare are lifted up no longer,
Natural disasters and man-made hurts are gone,
The black-haired people live robust and peaceful,
Profits and rich resources last for ever.
He makes rules and measures just and fair;
He is the regulator of all beings.
He exalts farming.
Vessels and tools have identical measurements,
Documents are written in a single script.
Everyone lives out his allotted span,
And there is no one but attains to his desires.

Source B
Cracking his long whip, he drove the universe before him, swallowing up the eastern and western Zhou and overthrowing the feudal lords. He ascended to the highest position and ruled the six directions, scourging the world with his rod, and his might shook the four seas.

(This is what Sima Qian wrote about Qin Shihuangdi in the *Records of the Grand Historian of China*. What sort of impression does it give of him?)

THE FIRST EMPEROR
1. What evidence is there that the Qin Empire was well organised?
2. What did Qin Shihuangdi do that showed he was a strong ruler?
3. What policies and actions made him feared?
4. Did the people benefit from his rule?
5. Why did he burn books?
6. Two contemporary comments were:
   'The country of Qin has abandoned morality. It has managed its officers by power and its people by slavery.'
   'Qin shares customs with the barbarians, delights in cruelty, and knows nothing of good faith or virtuous action.'
   Do these comments help you in your enquiry into the idea of a civilisation? Use the diagram on page 4 to help you shape your ideas. Write them down.

Chapter two

Qin Shihuangdi's underground army

Qin Shihuangdi's power is also revealed by his tomb which took several years to build. It is said to contain a map of China with moving rivers of mercury in the floor, and a map of heaven with all the known stars in the ceiling. Crossbows were set to shoot automatically at tomb-robbers. These secrets were known to the craftsmen who built it, and so they were walled up inside when the tomb was closed.

The discovery

In 1974 a well was being dug 1200 metres east of the outer wall of the Emperor's tomb, 64 kilometres from Xi'an, Qin's capital. Out of the ground appeared a soldier — a soldier of clay! Soon, from the red earth there emerged a whole army of terracotta figures, forming an unbelievable sight — an archaeologist's dream.

Gradually four pits were uncovered, similar to army camps.

Pit One: This was the largest and contained 6000 figures in military formation.
Pit Two: Excavated in 1976, this was L-shaped and contained 1400 chariots and cavalrymen, escorted by archers.
Pit Three: Excavated in 1977, and one-third the size of pit one, this contained an elite command force.
Pit Four: This was empty, maybe because of the unexpected death of the Emperor.

Archaeologists removing some figures from a pit

Terracotta soldiers formed up in one of the pits

A terracotta soldier with a horse. Notice how alert the horse appears to be.

The Army: On the alert...

This was no mass-produced army; each piece was individually created. No two faces were alike and many minority nationalities were included, suggesting that every soldier had sat for a portrait. The men and horses were originally coloured with paint, but most of this has faded. Traces indicate some interesting colour combinations, possibly defining ranks and regiments. All sorts of clues about this remarkable army become apparent when looking at the pieces. Here are a few:

- There are seven types of armour. For example, officers wear armour with decorations on shoulders, breasts and backs.
- The spearmen and the archers are all lightly clothed to permit speedy movement.
- Rank is also revealed by tassels and ribbons.
- The headgear is often ornate with double folds and ribbons for high ranks, whereas charioteers wear bonnets with strings, and cavalrymen have close-fitting caps painted yellow with red dots.
- No head-dress adorns the infantrymen whose hair is coiled in top-knots.

This army of clay seems well-prepared and has an atmosphere of energy and movement, with the alert horses shown by pricked ears and flared nostrils. What do you think is the purpose of this vast model army buried underground?

Two modern historians have commented on the army:

Source C
The scale and the sheer numbers of China's underground army testify to the power of the Emperor, who is said to have led 'a million armoured soldiers, a thousand chariots, and ten thousand horses to conquer and gloat over the world'.

(C. Blunden and M. Elvin in *Cultural Atlas of China*)

A close-up of two of the terracotta soldiers.

The head of a terracotta soldier.

EVIDENCE: THE UNDERGROUND ARMY

1. Imagine being an archaeologist in 1974 uncovering this army. A magical excitement would perhaps be present. What questions would you ask about these amazing finds?
2. What do you learn from the evidence on these two pages about:
   a the Emperor – his attitudes and power?
   b the army – its organisation, size and importance?
   c the soldiers – their ranks, uniforms, hair-styles, weapons and physical features?
   d the crafts people – their skills and materials?
   e the society under Qin Shihuangdi?
3. If you do the above work in note form you can now produce an archaeological report or booklet with illustrations about the underground army, using all your notes.

Chapter two

≡ Qin Shihuangdi and the Great Wall

A photograph of the Great Wall today. Notice the stark and hostile surroundings.

Apparently, the Great Wall is the only artificial structure that is visible from a spacecraft orbiting the earth!

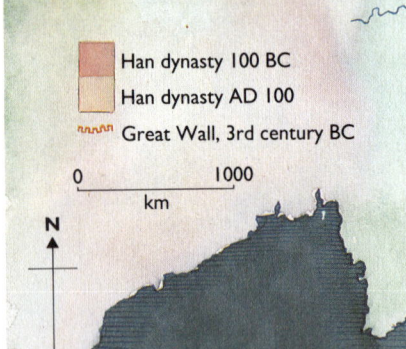

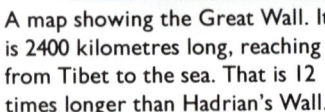

A map showing the Great Wall. It is 2400 kilometres long, reaching from Tibet to the sea. That is 12 times longer than Hadrian's Wall.

Qin Shihuangdi defends his empire

The Great Wall was started in 221 BC to defend the Qin Empire from the raiding northern nomadic tribes. It linked previous frontier fortresses, and stretched across wild steep country, up mountains and down valleys. Seven years in the building, some of the wall still stands today, though over the centuries it has been altered and re-built.

The wall was made of stone and clay. It stood higher than a double-decker bus, with watch-towers every 200 metres where beacons were lit to signal an enemy's approach. The stone-paved top could carry two chariots racing side by side, or eight men marching together. Soldiers spent all year there. In the wall a few huge well-guarded wooden gates, studded with iron nails, connected the main roads of China to caravan routes through the mountain passes and across the desert.

How was it built?

We marvel at how Stonehenge, the Pyramids, and the Great Wall were built, simply using human power, without mechanical aids like bulldozers and tractors. Thousands of peasants used buckets and ropes to haul, move and carry the earth and stones. They were forced for years on end to abandon homes, wives and children, to work on the wall. There was little food or shelter for them in the many wild, isolated and barren places that the wall was crossing. The northern winters were cold and long. Thousands died and were buried in the clay inside the wall. There is a story that a magician said that the wall would not be completed until 10,000 men were buried in it, so the Emperor found a man named Wen, meaning 10,000, and had him entombed alive in the wall! It was finished ...

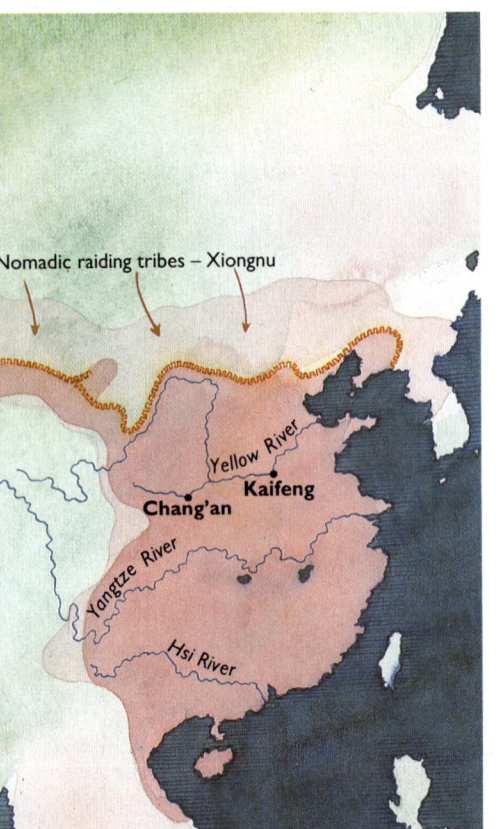

THE GREAT WALL

1. Now go back in time. You are one of Qin Shihuangdi's officials sent to check on the progress of the wall. Write a report for the Emperor. Praise his achievements, justify its construction and describe the work completed so far.
2. As one of the suffering peasants labouring on the wall, produce *either* a letter smuggled to your family, *or* a hidden picture with notes, conveying impressions of the wall, your work and conditions.
3. One day you may visit China and the Great Wall. Until you do (or in case you don't), using the information above, write and design a page for a present-day tourist guide to the Great Wall. Make sure you include its historical features.

A sad love-story of forced labour on the wall

Lonely and unhappy after her young husband had been taken away to work on the wall, Meng Chiang went in search of him. In a dream she pricked her finger, and the drops of blood made a trail to him. On waking she repeated what she had dreamed, and at last approached the wall. She saw some workers and she asked where her husband might be. (Read Source D.)

Just then, at the place where they were standing, the wall fell down. There was his body. She threw herself into the sea nearby. It is said that the wall has always been difficult to maintain at this point.

Source D

They answer, as sighs wring
Their hearts, 'Lady, let it be understood
This is Imperial ground.
Who would? Who could
Dare raise a burial mound? Here at the base
Of the Long Wall our brother's body lies.
Moved by our sense of common brotherhood
We have devoted to his memory
A three-foot stone, white, bearing on its face
Your husband's now immortal name to be
His tomb-tablet.'
The workers point, 'Here, see,
Just at this stone!'
Then to the group her eyes in question cling
'But here, in this abandoned, barren space,'
She puzzles,' Sirs, there is no sign or trace
Of any grave.'

PEOPLE IN THE PAST: THE EMPIRE OF QIN SHIHUANGDI

1. Use the evidence from pages 8 to 13 to complete the chart copied from page 7. Below are some suggestions.
2. Look at the timeline on page 7, and consider what was happening in Britain, and in Europe, at the time of Qin Shihuangdi. How does this compare with Qin's Empire and the lives of his people?
3. What features of Qin's Empire fit with your ideas so far that China was a civilisation? Why?
4. What features do not fit? Why?
5. Was China a peaceful country? Explain your answer. Add your findings to your wall display.
6. Find out what an obituary is. Gather some from newspapers, and discuss what they are aiming to convey about the dead person.
Now write the obituary of Qin Shihuangdi. Add a picture based on how you think he may have looked.

Does Marco Polo mention any of the things that are found in the Qin Empire? If you find any then you are discovering continuity from the past, from one period to another, that is, from the time of Qin right through to the time of Marco Polo.

Marco Polo may have simply failed to mention some of the things he saw, or changes may have occurred over time. Which do you think happened?

Was Qin Shihuangdi's Empire a civilisation?

For	Against	Comments
1 projects 2 uniformity 3 empire established etc...	methods of government burned books not always at peace etc...	

Summary: Was China a peaceful country?

In order to form some answers to this question you have looked at the Empire of Qin Shihuangdi. Further ideas on fair and peaceful rule will develop as you read more of this book.

Chapter three

What ideas were important in China?

Confucius

One man, called Confucius, helped to shape the ideas of China, just as, for example, Christ shaped the Christian world, and Muhammad shaped the Islamic world.

Confucius lived a long time even before Qin Shihuangdi. He lived in a troubled time of war, and for 14 years Confucius travelled from place to place pleading for peace and co-operation. The ambitious warlords who wanted more power would not listen, and so Confucius settled down to become a teacher of his ideas and beliefs. His books aroused the anger of Qin, because Confucius said the past was better than the present. Qin burned them but this did not wipe out his ideas.

What did Confucius say?

Confucius believed that people are basically good, and that any person can learn the right thoughts and behaviour, and can improve. A child learned to be good by obeying his or her parents and by showing a loving respect for them and so became a good adult. In return, it was the duty of parents to love and protect the children.

In this way, people could follow the Way of Heaven, and thereby find happiness. He believed it was more important to learn to live in the right way in this life rather than worry about what happens after death.

The Emperor and good government

According to Confucius an Emperor had to be wise and good, then his people would respect and obey him like a child obeys a parent. An Emperor was expected to follow the Way of Heaven. Then his rule would be blessed.

If an Emperor did not follow the Way of Heaven, crops would fail, the people would starve, and become dishonest.

Ordinary people could not share in government because that was the job of specially trained men. However, Confucius thought that an Emperor should listen to the complaints of his people, because then he could make them happy. If he did not listen, the people would be unhappy. In that case, Confucius said, find a *new* Emperor, by rebellion if necessary, and find one from a powerful and good family, whom the people could trust. It was their duty to do this because the Emperor had lost the approval of Heaven, and therefore the right to rule, by not behaving properly.

Confucius' real name was Kong Zi. The Latin name of Confucius was given to him in the seventeenth century by Catholic priests in Europe who found it easier to use, and the name stuck. He lived from 551 to 479 BC. This figure dates from the Tang Dynasty.

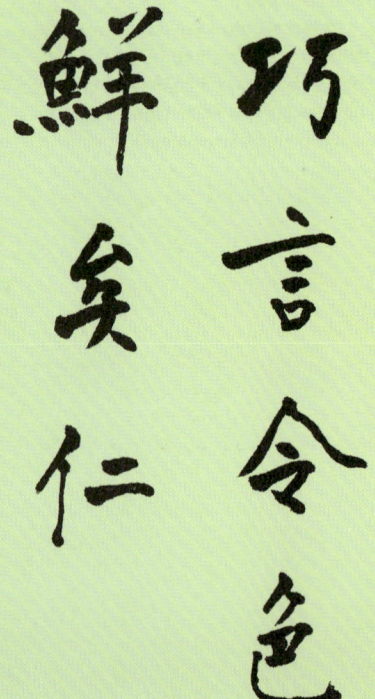

A saying of Confucius: 'Do not do to others what you would not have them do to you'

This is the Emperor T'ai-tsung of the Tang Dynasty

Other ideas

Daoism

Whereas Confucius' teaching had a practical side, Daoism was more mysterious. Dao means Way, and people who believed in these ideas thought that everything in the Universe followed a pattern or plan. Individuals had to find their way in this pattern, and stick to it, and then all would be well. Basically Daoists let everything take its course. They enjoyed life, and did not interfere in anything. Some of them became hermits or wisemen.

Buddhism

Buddhism was probably brought to China by traders from India and Central Asia. It was not welcomed by some people in China because Buddhists were expected to leave their families and become monks. More than 30,000 Buddhist temples were built, and more than four million monks lived in China. The temples provided plenty of work for painters and sculptors, and Buddhism also encouraged the invention of printing because so many copies of Buddhist prayers were required.

Buddhists believe that each creature is reincarnated after death in a higher or lower form of existence, depending on the quality of the last life, that is, whether it was good or bad. Thus they thought it was wrong to kill anything.

Popular Religion

Many Chinese had several beliefs, and mixed these three main ideas together with others.

- The ancient gods of wind and soil were worshipped.
- There was ancestor worship which established the endless chain of life.

The Chinese did not think that these beliefs contradicted each other; all played a role in uniting the people and were part of the balance of everything. This is explained by the saying, 'The three teachings flow into one'.

Buddha with some pupils. There is a story that the Emperor Ming of Han in AD 65 dreamed he saw an enormous god with a golden body and light shining round his head. One of his ministers said that it was a god called Buddha from the West. The emperor sent men to India to find out about Buddha, and statues and books about him were brought back to China. Buddha means 'enlightened one'. The original Buddha was a prince, Siddhartha Gautama, born in Nepal in 563 BC. After he had seen some terrible things, he became a monk, and thought about how people could escape their lives of misery.

A painting, *The Three Teachings*, with Confucius in the middle, Buddha in meditation on the left, and Lai Zi, the founder of Daoism, on the right.

PEOPLE IN THE PAST: CHINESE RELIGIONS

1. Why did ordinary people like Confucius' ideas?
2. Emperors could like and dislike Confucius' ideas. Why?
3. Why did the poor people like Buddhism?
4. Would Daoists make good soldiers or officials?
5. Why did Confucius' ideas last so long?
6. Do you think Confucius' ideas are a good basis for a government?

Chapter three

Medicine: The body and the universe

Learning about beliefs and ideas helps you to understand different aspects of Chinese life. The rest of this chapter looks at the impact of these beliefs. Medicine links with all the ideas you have read about so far. Even today Chinese hospitals offer ancient methods of treatment as well as modern methods like those practised in Western hospitals. The Chinese link sickness and treatment to their ideas of the whole world.

A visit to a Chinese doctor in the past

A healthy body was in balance with its own parts and with the natural world. Illness occurred when this balance was disturbed. The doctor's task was to restore the body to balance.

The doctor's diagnosis was in four parts:

- visual examination, especially the tongue
- listening to breathing, coughing, groaning; and smelling the breath, body odours, and excretions
- asking questions on medical history and conditions
- touching, especially the pulses. Ancient texts refer to 20 sensations for doctors to notice when feeling the pulse.

Acupuncture

Doctors could use acupuncture. This treatment was used from the second century BC onwards. It is the insertion of a fine needle into the body at certain points to affect the balance between the systems of energy in the body. Today 100 points in the body are still used, but ancient texts refer to several times more.

Surgery was opposed because cutting into the body would create a dramatic imbalance, and the body was also regarded as a gift.

Source A
We receive our flesh, bones, hair and skin from our fathers and mothers, and should on no account do anything to injure them.

(A text from the Han dynasty.)

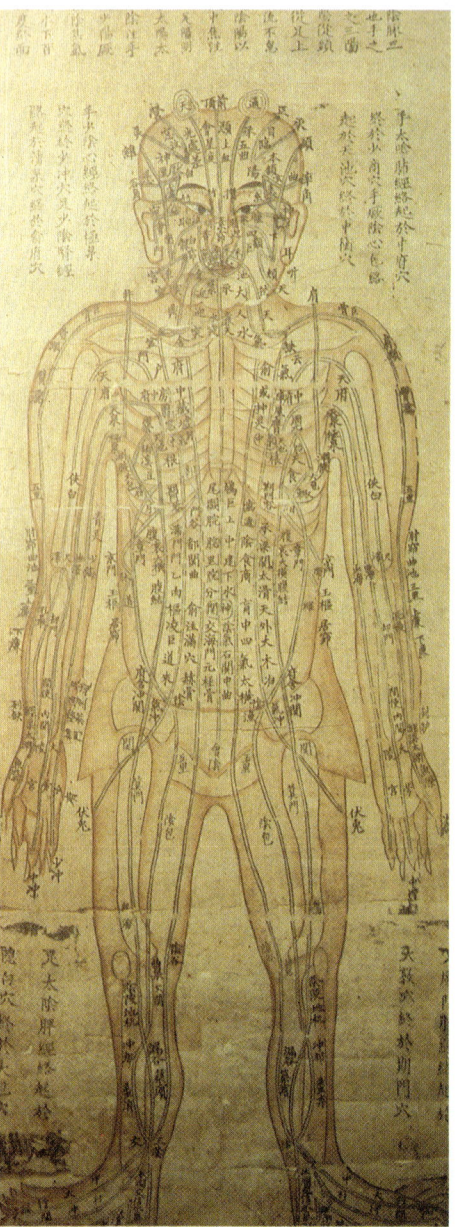

A Chinese acupuncture chart showing where the needles should be inserted

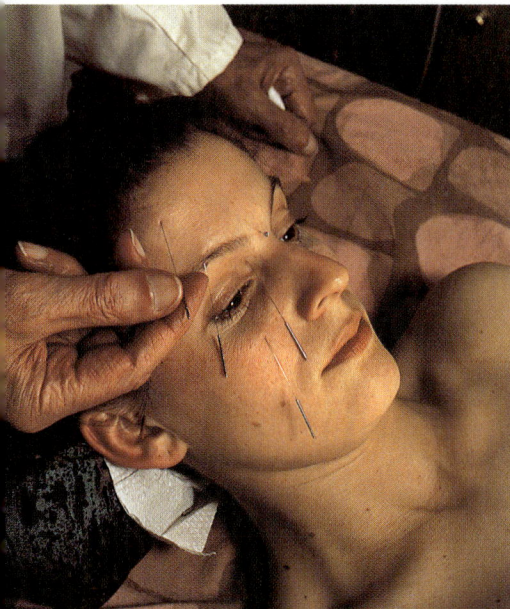

Circulation of the blood

From the second century BC Chinese doctors knew about the circulation of the blood. In 1628, 2000 years later, the idea was thought to be a breakthrough in Europe when William Harvey published his theory on the circulation of the blood.

Source B

The flow of the blood is maintained by energy, and the motion of energy depends on the blood; thus coursing in mutual reliance they move around. The system is of dykes and retaining walls forming a circle of tunnels which control the path that is traversed by the blood so that it cannot escape or find anywhere to leak away.

(Yellow Emperor's Manual)

The Chinese even removed blood vessels from corpses and laid them out to discover the distance travelled by blood in circulation: it was 17 metres. They also knew that the heart pumped the blood; classrooms contained bellows and bamboo tubes with liquid circulating to teach students about circulation and the heart.

Inoculation against smallpox

In the tenth century at the time of the Song dynasty, the eldest son of Prime Minister Wang Tan died of smallpox. Desperate to prevent other members of his family from catching it, Wang Tan summoned physicians, wisemen and magicians. A Daoist hermit came and brought the technique of inoculation. This is the giving of a live virus into the body, which then becomes immune to that disease. The danger is that the full disease will develop. The Chinese method to prevent smallpox guarded against this happening. Some poxy material was placed on a plug of cotton which was inserted into the nose, and thus absorbed through breathing. The poxy stuff was obtained from other people who had received this treatment and had developed a few scabs; it was not taken from dangerously ill people. In this way a weakened form of the virus was used.

What ideas were important?

The photograph on the left shows acupuncture today. This woman is having acupuncture treatment to try and stop her having persistent headaches.

MEDICINE

Use the information on these pages to fill in this chart. Summarise the differences and the similarities between traditional Chinese medicine and modern Western medicine.

	China	Western	Similarities/Differences
Knowledge of body			
diagnosis			
treatments			

Chapter three

The Han dynasty and the ideas of Confucius

You have seen how the Qin Emperor established his country and power, and how he started what is referred to as a civilisation. You may have questioned Qin's 'civilisation' because of his cruelty.

You also know that the Qin Dynasty of Shihuangdi did not last his hoped for 10,000 generations. The ideas of Confucius had a part to play in this. How and why did his Empire end?

NEWSFLASH...
209 BC 900 CONSCRIPT SOLDIERS EN ROUTE FOR THE FRONTIER TO CARRY OUT GENERAL DUTIES, BLOCKED BY FLOODS, KILL THEIR COMMANDER. THE REVOLT SPREAD, AND PEASANTS JOINED THE FIGHT.

From the Han Dynasty onwards, a dragon with five claws represented the Emperor. Chinese dragons were not fierce, but good-natured.

The rebels could have been executed for not carrying out orders. There must have been a lot of unhappiness and fear to encourage this rebellion. Within three years Qin's capital fell to Liu Bang who had led a group of soldiers. He took the title of Emperor. In this way the Han dynasty was founded and it lasted for 400 years, from 206 BC to AD 220, at the same time as the Roman Empire. The territory ruled by the Han Emperors was extended (see page 8) and China was generally at peace. The people became so proud of the Han dynasty that they regarded themselves as the only civilised country in the World. Even today the Chinese refer to themselves as the people of Han.

How did the Han dynasty create such pride?

At first the new Emperor, unused to his work, was rather rough and crude, until a minister advised him that he could not continue to 'rule on horseback', but must rule with care and consideration. So began the following:

- Schools were set up to teach the ideas of Confucius.
- The first university in the world was founded in 124 BC. Good graduates became trained officials who helped to rule the Empire.
- The same language and writing were used throughout China, and paper was invented in the second century AD.
- The Empire was divided into 18 provinces which were in turn sub-divided into a total of about 100 districts. Officials governed the provinces and districts so that local government was important to the people.
- The first of 24 dynastic histories was written about emperors, kings and ordinary people. This Chinese history is the longest in the World.
- Art, crafts and many other impressive inventions also occurred, which you will learn about in chapter 4.

This bronze model shows an important Han official in his carriage.

CAUSES AND CONSEQUENCES: THE BEGINNING OF THE HAN DYNASTY

Here are some statements linked with the rebellion of 209 BC.

- The peasants were tired and miserable because of the forced labour used to build the Great Wall, towns, canals and palaces.
- Continual demands for military service stopped them working on the land, and gathering their crops.
- The harsh laws and taxes affected everyone.
- Scholars were unhappy because of the restrictions on some books, and the burning of other books.
- Liu Bang was a skilful fighter.
- Confucius taught that an Emperor who was no longer being good, could be overthrown. The people could find a new Emperor.

1 a Are some of these more important than others in causing rebellion? Which ones do you think are more important? Explain your answer.
  b Do you think all the people would have the same motive for rebelling?
  c How would a follower of Confucius, justify this rebellion?
2 The first Han Emperor was advised not to continue 'to rule on horseback'.
  a What did this mean?
  b Did his new type of government prevent that?
  c Would Confucius have approved of the Han way of government?

Han craftsmen could create exquisite animal models. These leopards are bronze inlaid with gold.

Chapter three

Ideas, and law and order

Source C
Officials are leaders of the people, and it is right and proper that the carriages they ride in, and the robes that they wear should correspond to the degrees of their dignity.

(An edict of 144 BC)

The officials' role was very important for controlling the Empire. They were at the top of Chinese society.

Their badges of office were gold, silver and bronze, with purple, blue, yellow or black ribbons, according to the position and salary. The officials were paid in grain, coins or silk, and had one rest day in five.

They formed a Civil Service, with grades and promotions, and were responsible for education, military affairs, justice, collecting taxes in grain, textiles or cash, and for public works like road-building. They were very powerful. Some of them were even astronomers, who looked after the calendar, and interpreted the astrological signs. Most officials had to work away from home, sometimes in remote parts of the Empire, to limit corruption. Such a career offered many advantages and officials had to pass very difficult examinations. Officials recommended men for office who had education, could read and write, and knew Confucius' Classics.

Here is a letter that an official in Shangjun, near the border, **might** have written to his wife at their home in the Han capital Chang'an, in the year AD 150.

> My love,
>
> How I miss you and the children. At present I am looking at the mural in my study and reception room, but unfortunately it reminds me of you. Scenes of city life and the theatre are delicately depicted, and on another wall are painted acrobats and musical entertainments – all vivid memories of happy times we have spent so often in Chang'an. This town seems remote and lacks such relaxations. Outside the garden and lake are calm and serene, with the lotus blossoms in full bloom and heavy with scent; the birds sing, and the servants are very attentive, but I obtain little pleasure from them. I shall read Confucius tonight to gain reassurance.
>
> I suppose that I do look grand in my new silk robe with bronze emblem and purple ribbons; certainly I am respected. Yesterday I went by chariot to examine the canal-building, and the new road had been well-maintained by the forced labour. This morning I read several reports on the area and the likely amount in taxes it could raise for our illustrious Emperor. Tomorrow I shall begin drafting my first report on this area; increased trade would certainly improve it, and bring more wealth, but past attacks have left the people somewhat drained. Luckily the officials here seem very hard-working. Next week I may go hunting – the deer are apparently plentiful. I have an invitation from the magistrate who seems a fair man; I observed him settling a case the day after my arrival here. Tea is about to be served, and I expect the arrival of the astrologer who will guide me through the rest of the month. The official post will deliver this to you, and a present of silk will shortly arrive for you also. My leave cannot come too quickly. I shall write again soon.

What did the Chinese invent and create?

Chapter four

This chapter looks at the crafts and inventions of China. The variety, skill and range of these is amazing. Think about your investigation as you read about them.

Crafts

Here are just a couple of examples of craftsmanship. Look carefully at these two objects, and try to answer the following:

- What are the objects made of?
- What decoration do they have?
- Who might have owned them, and why?

We know about objects like these from archaeological finds. Tombs of the Han dynasty have yielded objects in jade, bronze and lacquer, as well as earthenware models of buildings, figures and scenes of farm life. For example, the family tomb of the Marquis of Dai (about 160–150 BC) in Henan contained three nestling coffins. Inside the inner coffin was the perfectly preserved body of a woman, probably his wife. There were also lacquer mugs and ladles for everyday use, and silk embroidered with twenty coloured threads. A later Han tomb contained more than two hundred objects, mostly of bronze, including the flying horse with one hoof on a swallow (see page 25).

Lacquer

'The most ancient industrial plastic known to man' is one description of lacquer. So what is lacquer?

- It is made from the juice of the lac trees of West, North-West and East China. The juice is refined, then applied to wooden surfaces or textiles and forms a most remarkable surface – so strong that hot water and acids cannot affect it, and excellent for engraving and painting with decoration.
- The Han craftsmen were very good at lacquerwork, making practical things like cups, plates, dishes, and things for the army like sword sheaths, shields, and parts of carriages.
- The production of lacquer objects was very well organised. There is a cup in the Musée Guinet in Paris that can be dated precisely to the year AD 4. How? There is an inscription on it which gives the date of manufacture, the names of the seven craftsmen making it, and the five officials who were involved in the production of it!

A lacquered wooden deer

Chapter four

A mottled white jade carving from the third century BC

The jade burial suit of a princess. In 1968 the tomb of a Han prince and his wife was opened. Among the many remarkable and magnificent objects were two jade suits of Prince Lui Sheng and Princess Dou Wan, his wife. Her suit was made of 2156 small, thin, square or rectangular wafers of jade, linked by gold thread through tiny holes in the four corners of each wafer. Each hole is only one millimetre in diameter and the saw used to cut the jade had a delicately fine blade. It has been calculated that an expert Han jadesmith would have taken more than ten years to complete such a suit.

Jade

Source A
There is warmth in jade's lustre and brilliancy, this is the manner of kindness; it may be broken but cannot be twisted, this is the manner of bravery.

(A dictionary in the second century AD)

Jade can be colourless or white, or range through the shades of greens, blues, reds, yellows, mauves, and browns. The Chinese treasured this stone — which is so hard that steel cannot cut it, and which is ice-cold to touch — as beautiful and desirable, and made in Heaven. They believed it could preserve the dead, and that it possessed healing powers. The Chinese used a special circular knife to cut through it, and then shaped it into exquisite objects. The skilled craftsmen used substances harder than jade, like crushed garnets, to carve it.

Porcelain

Source B

There is in China a very fine clay from which are made vases having the transparency of glass bottles; water in these vases is visible through them, and yet they are made of clay.

(An Arabic merchant, Suleiman, in AD 851)

So what was this remarkable material?

- Porcelain is the result of Chinese genius. It is hard, smooth, translucent (see-through) when made in thin pieces, and makes a bell-like sound when tapped. The plates from which we eat have these qualities and are therefore porcelain or 'china', whilst a flowerpot, for example, is earthenware.
- Porcelain is made from pure clay or kaolin, covered with a glaze, and fired at very high temperatures (1280°C). Its manufacture was a closely guarded secret. Marco Polo was not allowed to watch it, and even in the fifteenth century porcelain was very rare in Europe. It was finally made in Europe in the eighteenth century.
- A few intact pieces have survived from Tang times (618–906), but it was in the Song dynasty (960–1279) that its production increased, and beautiful pieces were created. All over the country were kilns employing thousands, and making porcelain in the famous single colours – purple, white (blanc de chine), and black and white.

A porcelain jug and basin

Metalwork

Both bronze and iron articles were made in China, either for a specific use or for decoration.

- Bronze bells, vases, dishes, spoons, incense-burners, and personal ornaments have all been found. Bronze was also used for minting coins and casting mirrors.
- By AD 1 to 2 there were about 48 iron foundries north of the Yangtze River, in the valleys of the Yellow and Huai Rivers, and in the Shantung Peninsula. These foundries made:
    - farming tools, for example, shares for ox-drawn ploughs, and heads for hoes,
    - domestic lamps, pots, and knives,
    - weapons such as swords, spears, helmets, armour, and arrowheads.

By now you may have been able to identify the objects on page 23, and answer the questions.

In case you were not sure, the round object is a lacquer plate with a dragon decoration. The other object is a bronze monster mask and ring. Only wealthy people could afford them.

A bronze 'flying horse' with one hoof on a swallow! It is only 30 centimetres high, and shows superb balance. It reveals the Chinese saying, 'a body as light as a swallow'.

Chapter four

Poetry and Literature

After the Tang dynasty fell in AD 906, the north was lost to barbarians, and the capital moved from Chang'an to Kaifeng further east. A new capital was set up for the Southern Song dynasty in 1127 at Hangzhou.

In the Song period (960–1279) the arts and culture flourished, and reached a high point, in spite of constant invasion threats from the 'barbarous hordes'. This is known as 'The Song Renaissance'.

The Song Renaissance

In the twelfth and thirteenth centuries the Chinese passion for learning developed into its Renaissance. Printing, art, literature, the past, and archaeological discoveries aroused the interest of art-lovers and experts. Catalogues, encyclopaedias and articles all appeared covering a range of subjects – flowers, geography, history, physics, coins, rocks and so on. Literature broadened – it was no longer just for the scholars, but now included the middle and lower classes. Storytellers, drama, puppeteers, and shadow-play became very popular. There was a repertoire of fantastic stories, Buddhist tales, crime and romantic stories.

Poetry

Poetry was important to many people. It circulated in the markets in the ninth century, and could be used to pay for wine and tea. Three famous poets were Li Bai (701–762) and his contemporary Du Fu, and Su Dongpo of the eleventh century. Many creative pieces – painting as well as poetry – were completed in a sort of trance, induced by music, alcohol, or dancing. Li Bai, famous for his drunkenness, died when tipsy, by falling out of a boat while embracing the moon. Source C is one of his poems, written in the traditional style, on this theme.

Su Dongpo was a scholar-official and an able administrator but he was never happy with politics, and in time he was exiled. When a prefect at Hangzhou, he had the West Lake cleared and drained, leaving a freshwater lake and wells for all the inhabitants, who were truly grateful to him. Here are two examples of his poetry – the first is very thoughtful whilst the second one, through the mouth of a peasant's wife, understands the suffering of the poor.

Source C
With wine I sit
absent to Night, till
(Fallen petals
in folds of my gown)

I stagger up
to stalk the brook's moon:
The birds are gone
and people are few.

This poem is translated and so some of its original meaning is lost.

The poet Li Bai after drinking too much wine, of which he was very fond.

Source D
Do you want to know what the passing
　year is like?
A snake slithering down a hole.
Half his long scales already hidden,
How to stop him getting away?
Grab his tail and pull, you say?
How could I hope next year won't come –
My mind shrinks from the failures it may
　bring.
I work to hold on to the night.
While I can still brag I'm young.

Source E
My tears are all cried out, but rain never
　ends.
We sold the ox to pay taxes, broke up the
　roof for kindling;
We'll get by for a time, but what of next
　year's hunger?
Officials demand cash now – they won't
　take grain;
The long north-west border tempts
　invaders.
Wise men fill the court – why do things
　get worse?
I'd be better off bride to the River Lord.

Painting

Another talent of the Chinese was painting. It was done on silk or paper, in the form of hanging scrolls, handscrolls, fans or album leaves. The paintings tended to be of four types.

Landscape: 'the single thread of heaven'. Landscapes were always of mountains and water, with humans small and irrelevant. The aim was to unite heaven and earth in a landscape, and when looking at such a painting it was regarded as a religious experience, with the viewer losing themself in the landscape and wandering freely, whilst at the same time remaining part of an ordered world.

Figure-painting. There remained a rich tradition of figure painting – of Confucian sages and virtuous people; of Buddist-influenced wall-paintings; and court paintings showing costume, posture, and social order. A good example of the latter is *The Night Revels of Hang Xizai*, painted about 923–36. The Emperor had heard of the nightlife of his Prime Minister, Hang Xizai, when singing girls and revellers crowded his apartments. Like a hidden camera, the court painter was sent by the Emperor to depict these scenes so that the Prime Minister could be challenged about his misdemeanours and bad behaviour.

Calligraphy. Literature and painting were not always separated; the two developed side by side during the Song period. A painting was often accompanied by a poem, conveying the same ideas or subject, whilst a poet was skilled with the brush because of the art of calligraphy. There could be no hesitation or revision; before putting brush to paper the essence of the subject must be grasped. The saying, 'The brush dances and the ink sings', captured this approach.

Decorative. By the twelfth and thirteenth centuries painting became more realistic and decorative. Ordinary objects of daily life – herbs, insects, flowers, birds, vegetables, carts, bridges and houses – became popular.

Chapter four

Gifts to the West

In the table on the right there are two dates for each remarkable invention. The first date defines the invention in China. The second date shows the Chinese invention's adoption, or its discovery, in Europe. The latter date is either precise to the year, or refers vaguely to a whole century. Why do you think this is so?

Invention	China	Britain and Europe
paper	2nd century BC	AD 1150
wheelbarrow	1st century BC	12th century AD
umbrella	4th century AD	AD 1600
printing – block	8th century AD	AD 1423
printing – movable type	11th century AD	AD 1456
playing cards and paper money	9th century AD	AD 1337 & 1661
segmental arch bridge	7th century AD	14th century AD
iron plough	6th century BC	18th century AD
chain pump	1st century AD	16th century AD
magnetic compass	4th century BC	AD 1190
kite	5th/4th century BC	AD 1589
gunpowder	9th century AD	AD 1330
silk	from about 1300 BC	AD 552–4
stirrup	3rd century AD	about AD 580

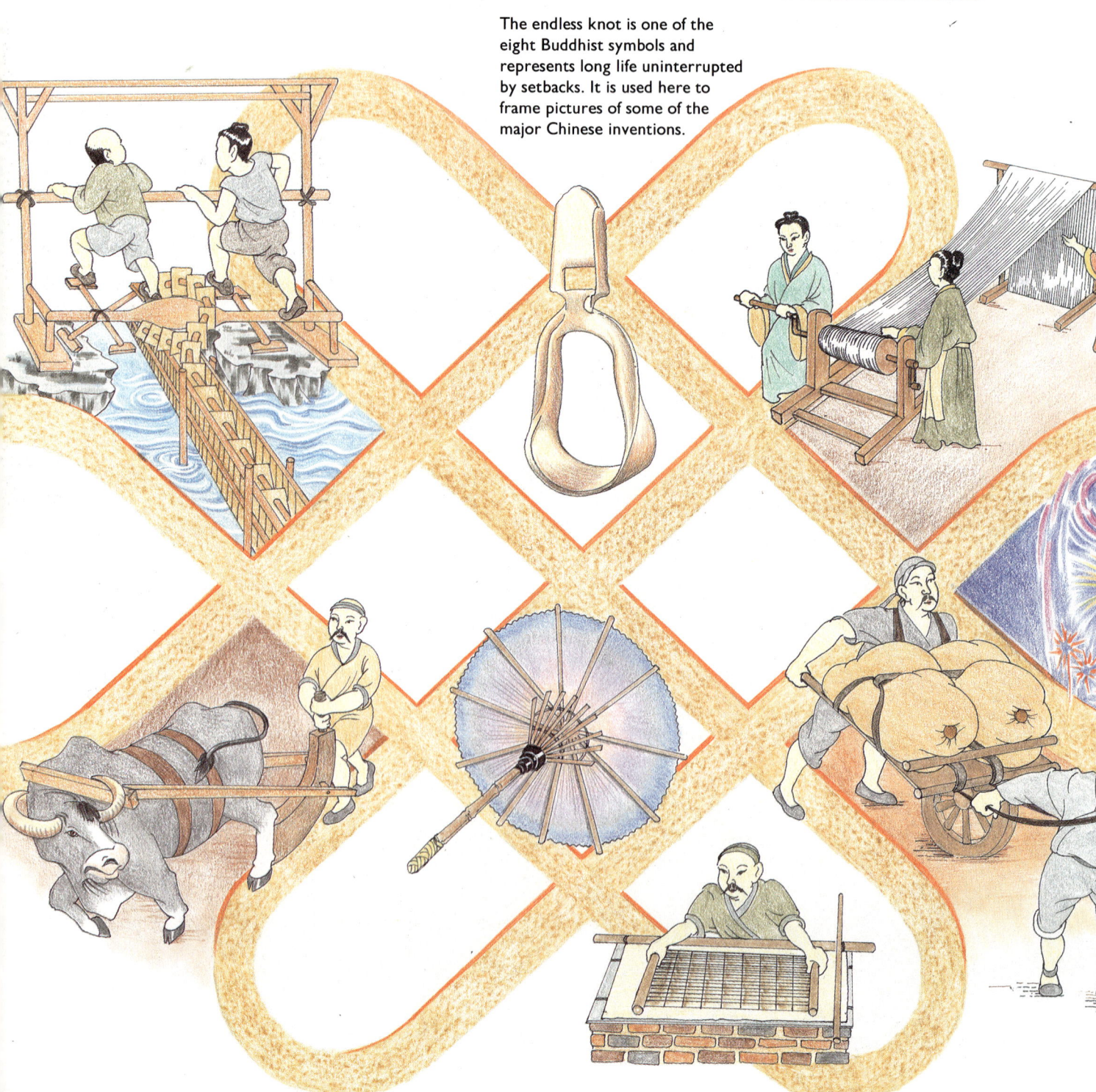

The endless knot is one of the eight Buddhist symbols and represents long life uninterrupted by setbacks. It is used here to frame pictures of some of the major Chinese inventions.

Many other things too ...

There are many other things that the Chinese invented or discovered before anyone else. The list seems endless. On the right are just a few more. You may find out about even more things.

Tea; porcelain; fireworks; crossbow; lacquer; chess; dominoes; matches; shadow-plays; sedan-chairs; minerals like zinc and coal; plants like peach and apricot trees, camellia, peony and others; winnowing machine; rudder and so on ...

Chinese inventions 29

PEOPLE IN THE PAST: CRAFTS, INVENTIONS AND DISCOVERIES

1 Place the inventions and discoveries in the table into categories – domestic; engineering, agriculture, transport, warfare, and others. Add two dates for each – one for its invention in China, the other for its use in Europe.
   a Work out the time difference between the two dates. What conclusions can you form from this comparison?
   b Work out some reasons why these inventions were not known in Europe for a long time after their invention in China.
   c Why do you think the phrase 'Gifts to the West' is the expression used to describe the adoption of Chinese inventions in Europe?
   d Which of the inventions and discoveries do you think were most important and useful as 'Gifts to the West'?
   e Are there any which you think were not useful or relevant in Europe? Why?
2 What do all the things – crafts, artistry and inventions – on pages 23 to 29 tell you about the people of China and the type of society and country in which they lived?
   To assist you in answering this, consider the following:
   • the development of paper and printing and their effects,
   • the range of leisure-type inventions and creations,
   • the inventions linked with agriculture and transport.
3 Think of the civilisation diagrams on page 4 and on page 7, and the ideas you have so far on China. How does everything in this chapter contribute to the idea of China as a civilisation? Add to your developing, and by now very interesting, wall display.

This is a Chinese earthquake recorder from AD 132! Each dragon's head has a ball held in its jaws. Inside there is a weight attached to a series of levers. The movement caused by an earthquake makes one of the balls fall out into a frog's mouth. The ball which falls shows the direction where the earthquake shock originated.

Summary: What did the Chinese create and invent?

Many of the world's most important inventions came from China. By the time that the invention of paper passed to Western Asia and Europe in the eighth century, the Chinese had developed printing, and this did not reach Europe for another 700 years! Such inventions brought reading and writing to ordinary people. The Chinese were the first to understand magnetism, and they used the compass for navigation a thousand years ago. Europeans later adopted it and explored the whole world. In many areas, including iron and steel making, ship and bridge-building, the study of astronomy, and the manufacture of porcelain, the Chinese were centuries ahead of Europe. The simple wheelbarrow was used in China one thousand years before it came to Europe, and even today the versatile and ingenious Chinese wheelbarrows are not appreciated!

Chapter five

How did the people live?

So far you have looked at the government, ideas and achievements of China. Now you are going to read about more ordinary things and everyday life of the people, most of whom worked on the land. As you look at these pages try to work out whether the people lived civilised lives.

Life on the land was different in the North than in the South. The contrast between these two areas was great because of the two main rivers – the Yellow River in the North, and the Yangtse in the South. The environment of these two areas has not changed over the centuries.

三 The North

A boat on the Yellow River

Source A
The boats of the Yellow River are like slices of cut melon.
(Thirteenth-century poet)

- The Yellow River gets its name from the yellow dust which is carried by winds from the northwest. This dust covers everything, and makes life difficult.
- For three months in the winter the ground is frozen for more than 30 centimetres. Rainfall is low apart from in the three summer months, when heavy rain makes the river flood easily. This can sweep away the crops. Dykes are crucial to control this. However, the dust and flood water does make the immediate land fertile.
- Work is intense in certain seasons – ploughing, sowing, reaping of millet and wheat – whilst at other times work is impossible.
- Animals like oxen are kept, and pastureland lies to the north of the river.
- The boats are as described in Source A – slender and shallow – to carry light loads for short journeys. The river either flows at great speed after heavy rain, or is almost dry.

This is the North of China today. The intensely cultivated hillsides are prominent. This has not changed for centuries.

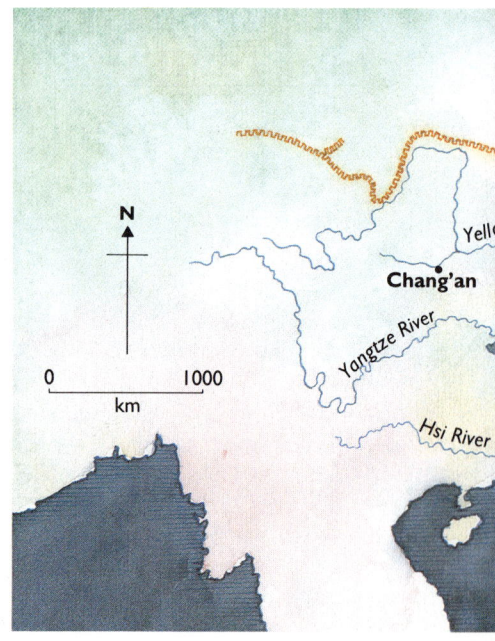

The South

Source B
The boats of the Yangtze are oval, like turtles, with tucked-in heads.

(Thirteenth-century poet)

- South of the Yangtze River is warm, with many lakes and rivers, and the people have always lived close to the water.
- The broad-based ships of the Yangtze carry heavy cargoes for many kilometres. The Yangtze is navigable for 2600 kilometres for small craft, and for over 320 kilometres for seagoing vessels.
- These boats 'like turtles' are the homes of families who spend most of their lives afloat.

Source C
Sailing along the creeks and waterways is the equivalent of cultivating vegetable gardens. Their fields are, so to speak, the middle of the lakes.

(A ninth-century northerner)

- The land is flat, enjoying a mild climate with light rain falling continually in the winter and spring, so agricultural work is continuous. Rice fields, with villages along the narrow dykes which separate the paddy fields and which serve as wheelbarrow paths and footpaths, create an endless pattern.
- Terraces – that is cultivated ledges on the hillsides – are made for other crops.
- Silk-farming and fish-farming combine effectively. The mulberry trees – the leaves of which are the food for the silk-worms – grow around the edge of carp ponds. The carp feed on the silk-worms' droppings.
- Citrus fruits, dates and chestnuts are easy to grow. Lac trees and bamboo groves are popular and hemp is grown for the coarse cloth of peasant clothes. Horses, cattle, sheep and pigs are also raised in the villages.
- Near the towns, market gardeners produce things like leeks and ginger.

How did the people live?

Notice how the two rivers – the Yellow and the Yangzte – divide the land.

A town in the South of China today, showing the timelessness of life there

The flooded paddy fields, where the rice is grown in the South

Chapter five

Village homes were usually a single courtyard with the main building positioned to the north, and other outbuildings like a pigsty nearby. The buildings were wooden with bamboo frames, and had a thatched or tiled roof. There was little privacy. Stone, which was regarded as a noble material for carving and ornamentation, was reserved for bridges, roads, paving for city streets, dykes, ramparts and Buddhist towers.

This Han pottery model was found in a tomb. It shows a pen full of sheep.

Everyone in the village, except the old, lame and infirm, worked from dawn till dusk to cut, thresh, dry and store the rice at harvest time. Children looked after the buffaloes and fed the animals in the yard (pigs, chickens and sometimes edible dogs) throughout the year, as well as gathering scarce firewood and collecting water from the well. In the winter some villages had schools where the children could learn the basics of writing and arithmetic.

What was peasant life like?

There has to be much guesswork about peasant life in China, because there are nothing like the records of the medieval villages of Europe. There are a few official handbooks for peasants on how to grow the best crops, and some tomb objects, but much is assumed because peasant life has changed very little over the centuries.

Peasant order

Farmers were very skilful. Their work was very detailed – more like gardening than farming. They relied on knowledge of local soils, weather, plants and fertilisers, especially in the rice fields. They grew huge amounts of food.

Work on the land and its crops resulted in close family and village life. The head of the family and village elders were respected and this resulted in peace in the countryside for much of the time. The peasants were too busy providing food for the family, paying taxes, and avoiding forced labour, to be troublesome. In return the peasants were protected by the Emperor's government. Several Han edicts open with, 'The world is based on agriculture,' showing how valuable village life was to China's peace and prosperity.

Peasant disorder

Poverty was real and could be caused by harsh taxes. This poem by a Song poet expresses this:

Source D
They do not grudge tending the rice in spring
But fear the payment of taxes in the autumn;
The evil officials act like sparrows or rats
And the thieving clerks like locusts or caterpillars;
They take extra with their enlarged measures.
People cannot avoid being flogged to make them pay up
And are further oppressed with private debt;
No smoke rises from the abandoned homesteads,
Never once in their lives have they tasted
Rice clean and bright as the cloudstone;
Those who eat it are always the idle
The mouths who grow it are forever watering.

Rebellion could result from harsh taxes, forced labour, and floods and droughts. In a crisis peasants often fled from their villages and beggars would roam around. The government lost taxes and had to hand out tools and seeds to assist the people in returning to normal life. At such times the peasants might rebel.

Peasant Calendar

A short text on peasant life survives from about AD 100 to 170 and gives an ideal view of twelve months. Here are some of the tasks.

1st month
New Year's Day: keep the festival. Purify themselves before offering strong drink to the shrine of their ancestors; pray for happiness and prosperity.
There are few jobs so send the boys to school.
Transplant trees like lac, bamboo, pine and oak.
Sow melons, gourds, onions and garlic.
Sweep up decayed leaves, and manure the fields.
Prune the trees and break up heavy ground.
Visit social superiors.

2nd month
Offer leeks and eggs to lord of the soil and spirits of the seasons.

3rd month
Practise archery in case of robbers.
Repair gates and doors; replaster walls and apply coat of lacquer. Break up the arable land soil, and light sandy soils.

5th month
Cut hay and collect firewood because the rains will soon make the paths too muddy to use.
Put bran for animal fodder in the winter in sealed jars to keep out maggots.
Collect herbs.

6th month
Textiles spun by the women; later the women dye the cloth and make it into clothes.

8th month
Cut hay, and offer leeks and eggs to lord of the soil and spirits of the seasons.
Present piglets and millet to the ancestral graves.

9th month
Check weapons, and prepare for the needs of the sick and orphans in the coming winter.
Repair granaries and storage pits.

10th month
Women work on the hemp and make sandals.

12th month
Pay visits to social superiors.
Slaughter pigs and sheep; fast and purify themselves, and offer wine to their ancestors.
Assemble the plough; feed the oxen well, ready for the next year.

For the first eight months of the year crops are grown and tended. All year brewing and preserving takes place.

EVIDENCE: PEASANT LIFE

1. Would you have preferred to live and work in the North or in the South of China? Write a letter to a friend being educated in a city who is missing village life explaining your choice by reference to the evidence.
2. For the area that is **not** your preference, present an official report to encourage people to live and work there. Include its special features, problems and contrasts.
3. a What impressions of peasant life do you get from the peasant calendar?
   b How useful is it as evidence?
   c What other aspects of peasant life would you like to learn about that are not mentioned here? Explain why.
4. a What do you think this peasant saying means: 'The collective earth is an orphan; the private plot is a child.'
   b Does the information on pages 30 to 33 support this saying?
5. Using the civilisation chart on page 7, decide whether this evidence for peasant life adds to, or reduces, the idea of China as a civilisation.

Chapter five

三 What was life like for women in China?

Source E

How sad it is to be a woman!
Nothing on earth is held so cheap.
Boys stand leaning at the door
Like gods fallen out of heaven.
Their hearts brave the four Oceans,
The wind and dust of a thousand miles.
No one is glad when a girl is born;
By her the family sets no store.

This poem was written in the third century AD. What do you learn from it about attitudes to girls and boys? Do these attitudes surprise you?

Foot-binding

In north and central China foot-binding was performed from about the age of five. The feet were bent back and very tightly bandaged until the bones of the instep were broken. It was agonising. The effect was that girls and women could only hobble. A fashionable foot was only eight centimetres long. This idea lasted until this century.

Why was this done? It began amongst court dancers as a way of performing light steps, though it eventually killed the art of dancing because it was too painful and the feet were too tiny. The rest of society copied it, except for the lowest class of women and the most southern parts of China. Was it to distinguish Chinese ladies from the 'barbarians' who surrounded China? What do you think?

It certainly prevented women from being active. Before it was popular there is evidence of travelling women traders, female polo players, and businesswomen like the Daoist nun Huang who pioneered the Lower Yangtze cotton industry. But not after this torture began.

Girls, the family and marriage

A boy was highly valued, whereas girl babies were often drowned at birth by the midwives or sold as servants if born to a poor family. After marriage a young woman transferred her loyalty to her in-laws. She might never see her parents again. Marriages were arranged. It was rare for a bride to have seen her future husband before marriage. A wife was subordinate to her husband and to older women like her mother-in-law. Obedience to them and the new family was a most important virtue.

Marriage occurred early for women, at about the age of 17. The age of the husband varied depending on his wealth, though the age gap could not be too great because the crossing of generations was not accepted. A wealthy man could take more wives. However, a woman with a strong personality could have a lot of influence over the family. The household budget and organisation were her responsibility, as was the upbringing of her children, and in time, her grandchildren. All of them were taught to obey her and never dispute her decisions. She chose punishments for them if they misbehaved. After death, women were worshipped as wives and mothers, not as individuals.

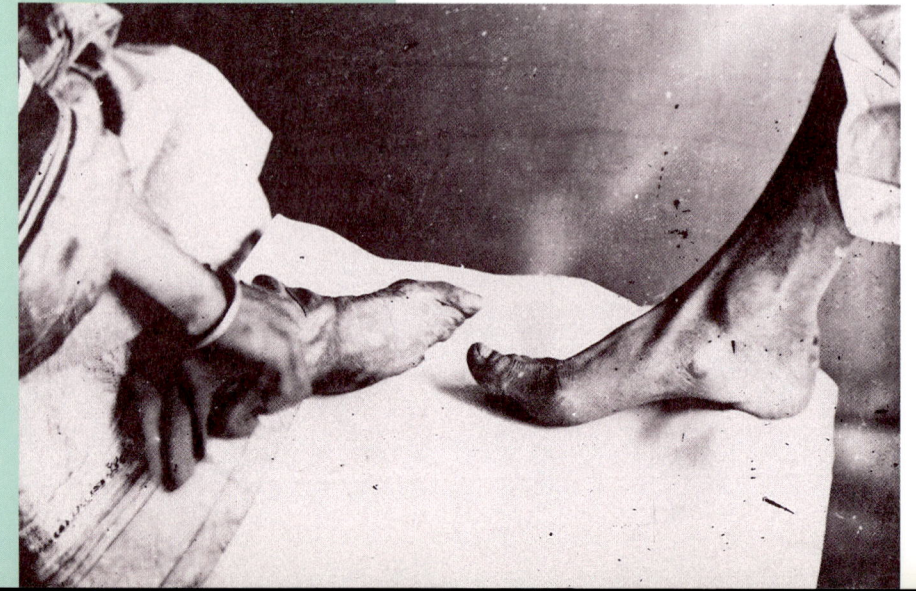

Here a Chinese woman in 1871 has unbandaged her foot, which had been bound since she was small, to compare it with a normal foot for the photographer.

Poor women

After marriage poor women were often engaged in small businesses like dressmaking and midwifery. The labour of peasant women was required throughout the year, and all processes in silk manufacture needed the active participation of women. The river women of the south and of the coast, who were engaged in work like transport and fishing, were never foot-bound. They ran the boats, rowed, cooked, sailed, and so on. Northern women referred to them as 'big-footed women' which was meant as an insult.

Women musicians

Two stories about women

- In many novels and operas women were depicted as strong. For example, Mulan was a popular opera heroine in the fifth and sixth centuries. Her family had to supply a soldier in a war against the barbarians, but with an old father and a young brother, she chose to go instead, dressed as a man. She became a general! When the war ended she changed back into her women's clothes to her soldiers' amazement.
- The Tang Emperor Xuanzong fell in love with Yang Guifei. She could play the lute and danced in a ballet called 'The Rainbow Skirt, Kingfisher Jacket', and the Emperor accompanied this on his drums. She loved lichi which could only be obtained 2400 kilometres from the capital. He had them brought fresh by fast relays of horses, and in this way the postal system began because people sent messages with these fast horses. The Emperor spent too much time with her and neglected his duties. Her relatives and favourites were given high and important positions. The Emperor trusted one of them as a frontier commander, but this caused a revolt against the Emperor in 756. The guards who escorted the Emperor on his flight from the capital persuaded him that it was Yang Guifei's fault, and they hanged her by a roadside temple. A poet retold this story, *The Everlasting Sorrow*, with much sympathy for her.

WOMEN IN CHINA

1. As a lord write an introduction to a book justifying the position of women in China.
2. Use the evidence to answer these questions:
   a Who had more freedom – a married lady or a single woman?
   b Who had the happier life – a married lady or a single woman?
3. Look back to page 3 to see what Marco Polo said about Chinese women. How far do his comments agree with the evidence on these pages?
4. How far do you think the ideas of Confucius influenced the attitudes to women and marriage?
5. Consider the civilisation chart on page 7, and decide whether the evidence on women in China contributes to your views on China as a civilisation.

How were the children educated in China?

Childhood could be a very happy time; punishments were few, and there were lots of toy and sweetsellers in the towns. Children were brought up to be gentle, obedient and friendly, and they were encouraged to live on good terms with relatives, friends and strangers, and to respect all elders.

Poor children remained illiterate, whilst the sons of the wealthy had a private tutor before going on to school. The boys in the towns learned the basics of reading and writing, and how to use an abacus. After the tenth century more people were educated because printing produced more books. It was rare for a girl to receive any education. Occasionally a father would teach his daughter, but the arts of spinning, embroidery, and playing musical instruments were the skills that were valued.

A typical school in Han times

Where?
The capital city – Chang'an.
Who?
Sons of highly placed families and sons of officials. Boys of promise from lower backgrounds were chosen by some officials to be educated in the capital.
Curriculum?
Many hours were spent mastering the written characters. Word-lists were compiled to assist in this. The texts of the classics were closely studied. The theory and practice of mathematics was also necessary.
Purpose?
To train future officials for the Civil Service.
Result?
Improved character by correction of faults and repression of ignoble motives, and exploitation of natural talents. Recognised as a scholar.
Future?
Nomination for a lower official's post, and then an examination by the senior officials in the capital or even by the Emperor himself. If successful, the award of a first, second or third class grade, and then a long wait for a vacancy. Sometimes up to a thousand men were waiting.

Civil Service examinations

By the time of the Song dynasty (960–1279) the only way to become an official was to pass the Civil Service examinations, which lasted in China until 1905. The idea was copied in the nineteenth century for the British Civil Service.

There was no age limit, and some men repeated the ordeal year after year. On the appointed day in the spring men went to the capital equipped with ink, brushes, and food. The examinations usually lasted three days. Each candidate was put into a numbered cubicle where he wrote his answers and ate his food – a type of solitary confinement. If anyone died, the corpse was hoisted over the wall! The examination comprised essays on the meaning of lines from one of the classics. Each essay was graded. Only about one per cent of the candidates were successful. Most entrants were financed by their families, showing the value placed on success.

The official's job

At work officials received reports from colleagues, interviewed the public, completed tax records and made suggestions to superiors. There was a strict hierarchy, and recognition of who was above and who below in the career structure. This resulted in a lot of ceremonies and rules of etiquette, like the kowtow, which was to bow as low as possible with the head touching the floor, in front of a superior.

Every three years a report was written on an official by his superior. It was fairly basic, and often required simply filling in the gaps.

Such a report might be followed by promotion or demotion. All this resulted in the large majority of officials working honestly and with a conscientious devotion to duty.

How did the people live?

There were a few stories of corruption: a building project in 80 BC required 30,000 carts of sand and gravel to be moved by hired oxen. This had been calculated at 1000 coins for each load. A high official indicated in the records that 2000 coins per load had been paid, thus making a profit of 30 million coins for himself!

CAUSES AND CONSEQUENCES: EDUCATION IN CHINA

1. Why did parents want to send their sons to a school like the one on page 36?
2. a Using the evidence fill in the chart to decide the effects of this type of education and career structure.
   b Is one of these effects more important than the others? Explain your answer.
3. Read Marco Polo's comment on page 3, beginning with, 'The natives of Hangzhou are men of peace ...' Was this because of the type of education that the men had received, or would other factors contribute to this outlook upon life? Explain your answer.
4. a How would you describe your education? Think of the subjects that you study plus all the other things you do at school.
   b What values and attitudes are you acquiring? How?
   c How far is your character being shaped by your education? Do other things count?
   d How far is your future being shaped by your education? Do other things contribute?
5. How did education make a contribution to China as a civilisation?

	gave unity to the people by ...	prevented new ideas and change by ...	encouraged curiosity about the world and ideas beyond China by ...
education			
career structure			

An official in court dress

Chapter five

How did the people of China enjoy life?

Food

Food played a large part in celebration of family events and annual festivals. This partly accounts for the excellent reputation and variety of Chinese food, which was much praised by poets and writers. The peasant tradition contributed as well. The constant threat of famine resulted in everything that was edible – vegetable, insect or offal – being used. The ox was essential to the peasant so beef was not eaten, and without dairy farming there was no milk or cheese. Just about everything else was consumed. Even human flesh was served in some restaurants in Hangzhou, and referred to as 'two-legged' mutton! The flesh of old men, women and children was served in separate dishes because the flavour varied.

The wealthy ate food with spoons and chopsticks which was served on a low table in small porcelain dishes, and brought in on lacquer trays. Variety and the number of dishes was more important than quantity. Rice-wine was served tepid with each dish. The only other drink was tea, made popular in Tang times having been introduced to China in the Han dynasty. There were very many varieties: Hangzhou produced three – Jewel, Forest of Fragrance, and White Clouds. Most were imported from elsewhere. Tea-drinking was regarded as an experience, producing a state of well-being. On the practical side, it was far better to drink tea in Hangzhou than the water which came from the Lake and was not always pure.

There were regional differences just as there are today in China. In the south people ate mainly rice, fish and pork, with mild flavours, though garlic, peppers, oyster sauce and black beans gave more robust tastes. Shark's fin and even snakes were added. In the north the food was stir-fried, with noodles, pancakes and steamed rolls also being offered.

Read this description of a Hangzhou restaurant by J. Gernet writing in 1962, but based on primary evidence. Eating seems both a serious affair and a pleasure.

Source F

The big restaurants had doors in the form of archways decorated with flowers. From them was suspended half a pig or a side of mutton. The decoration was brightly coloured. 'As soon as the customers have chosen where they will sit, they are asked what they want to have. The people of Hangzhou are very difficult to please. Hundreds of orders are given on all sides: this person wants something hot, another something cold, a third something tepid, a fourth something chilled; one wants cooked food, another raw, another chooses roast, another grill. The orders, given in a loud voice, are all different, sometimes three different ones at the same table. The waiter never mixes them up, and if by any unlikely chance he should make a mistake, the proprietor will launch into a volley of oaths addressed to the offending waiter, will straightway make him stop serving, and may even dismiss him altogether.'

There were restaurants where all the dishes, including fish and soups were served iced. Others specialised in certain kinds of food or in regional cooking of some kind. Others again, of the cheaper variety, only served noodles stuffed with vegetables or pork and beanshoots with boiled leeks. It is scarcely astonishing that the people of Hangzhou were often accused of being greedy.

This is a nineteenth-century Chinese painting of a marriage feast. Look at the decoration used.

Festivals

The Chinese have always had a passionate delight in festivals. They offered entertainment to everyone, of all ages and classes, and also got rid of worn-out 'breaths', diseases, and demons, and started a new and lucky period. There were a great many festivals throughout the year, for example, a festival of flowers, of the moon, of the dead, of the harvest, of the autumn, of weaving, of the birth of Dao, of the birth of Buddha, of chrysanthemums.

Festival of New Year

Rich and poor alike prepared dishes of vegetables and soya beans for the god of the hearth, who visited heaven at New Year to give a report on family members. Shops sold paper streamers and painted images of the door gods. Hawkers sold sweets and firecrackers (bamboo filled with gunpowder). Charms were nailed to the doors with red streamers placed above to 'welcome the spring'. At night-time everyone stayed inside to make sacrifices to their family ancestors and to all the guardian spirits of the house – gods of the door, of the stove, of the bed, of the courtyard. On New Year's Day there was calm in the streets and the shops were closed.

This was followed soon afterwards by the Feast of Lanterns which was the happy side of celebrating New Year. It lasted for three days and three nights, and it fell at full moon. The doorways of every house were now draped with embroideries and lamps, everywhere was lit up – squares, lanes and shops. There was much competition to decorate the best lantern. The finest ones were 100 to 130 centimetres in diameter, made of glass in five colours and painted with landscapes, people, flowers, bamboo, birds and furry animals. Games were played, and troupes of dancers, acrobats and musicians gave shows in rich people's houses. Everyone carried lanterns, and thoroughly enjoyed themselves.

Entertainments and leisure

Chess, calligraphy and literary composition were popular amongst the upper classes. Physical activities were reserved for the lower classes, or for the military, who played polo, football and practised archery and fencing. Entertainments like puppet-shows, acrobats and storytellers were a regular feature of street life.

This is the Festival of Agriculture, which was held in the spring.

Here we can see women musicians, together with acrobats and an early fairground ride!

Kites

For centuries kites have been made by the Chinese using bamboo for the frames and silk for the covering. Legend has it that a scholar and adviser to a Han Emperor first devised a kite to frighten off enemy forces attacking the palace walls. By putting sounding devices inside a light bamboo structure, he produced an eerie floating object that the wind caught, sending moaning, wailing voices into the night. The enemy, thinking the gods were warning them, left. Another use was in 549 AD 549 when messages were sent from within a besieged city to friends outside by means of kites.

The Chinese went on to make their kites for pleasure in the shapes of dragons, birds, insects and other creatures. Kite-fights were popular, the aim being to cut the string of one kite with the other's string.

FOOD, FUN AND FESTIVALS

1 Using the evidence on pages 38 and 39 describe a visit to a restaurant at festival time.
2 Design your own lantern or kite using decorations which the Chinese would have liked.
3 What does this amount of pleasure and entertainment tell you about;
   a the people?
   b the society?

DID THE PEOPLE OF CHINA LEAD CIVILISED LIVES?

1 Which aspects of everyday life in this chapter do not support the view that China was a civilisation? Why?
2 Which features do support the view? Why?
3 Summarise your thoughts. The people of China did/did not lead civilised lives because . . . This can also go with your wall display.

☰ Summary: How did the people live?

In this chapter on everyday life you have learned about different, but nonetheless important, features of China. These were the hardships but essential work of the peasants, the role of women, the value of education, plus the available pleasures of ordinary life. Such things give you a fuller picture of Chinese society.

How important was trade?

Trade (the exchange and purchase of varied goods) is an aspect of China that also needs investigating. Trade took place in the cities and ports. Goods travelled in and out of China by rivers, canals, the seas and overland.

六 What were the cities like?

Estimates vary as to how many people lived in cities and towns. In Han times calculations range from 18 million to 6 million, that is, from one-third to one-tenth of the total population. Unfortunately, many of the meticulous census returns from the Tang and Song times, detailing everyone with age, job, and the nature of the area, have been lost.

Towns varied in size and were usually an administrative centre, market place and centre of communications. Some were military bases, and others were industrial centres for salt, metals or textiles. Most had walls and followed a formal design, conveying an idea of the regularity of life, and that everything was ordered within the universe. In the thirteenth century Hangzhou had at least one million people living in 20 square kilometres, whilst contemporary European cities could not compare: London and Paris had 25,000 and 50,000 inhabitants respectively.

A plan of Chang'an, the Tang capital. It was a huge city of one million people, with over a hundred temples, and more than a hundred merchant trading guilds. It also had many markets selling both ordinary and exotic goods. Coins have been found from the Middle East.

It was also the Han capital from 202 BC to AD 8. In 81 BC a government debate took place about the hardships of the ordinary people. Officials took the opportunity to comment on many areas of life. Thus criticisms of town life appeared, especially of how the wealthy lived, such as the following:
- multi-storey homes with rich furnishings
- clothes of silk, furs and plumes
- too much meat and lavish meals with fancy dishes
- carriages with silver and gold fittings
- five-piece orchestra in the houses
- fancy funerals
- well-fed pets
- performing animals, tiger fights, puppetry and foreign girls

Chang'an: Tang and Han capital

Public buildings:
- palace
- market
- government office

Residential districts:
- low class
- middle class
- high class

1 Imperial palace
2 Great granary
3 Western market
4 Eastern market
5 Main pleasure quarter
6 Imperial observatory
7 Administrative city

A scene from Kaifeng, the Northern Song capital from 960 to 1126. Study this scene and see what you think of this city life. Notice the two-storey buildings which are the restaurants, the crowd around the storyteller, the shops, and all the other activities.

Kaifeng: Song capital until 1126

This city was famous for its bustling market places, and its 72 restaurants open day and night. Scenes from Kaifeng were painted by Zhang Zeduan in about 1100 on a very long scroll of paper called, *'Life along the river during the Spring Festival'*.

Hangzhou: Song capital from 1127

It became the capital after Kaifeng fell to the barbarians, and it was perfect – safe from invasion, ideal for trade, and with very attractive scenery. Canals throughout the city were vital for transport and movement, as well as sedans, horses and carts for passengers. Restaurants, taverns, tea-houses and shops remained open at night. There were shops for everything: repairers of ovens and knife sharpeners; firms providing everything for weddings and funerals; stores of luxury goods from India and the Middle East; and other shops galore for noodles, fruit, thread, incense, candles, oil, soya sauce, fish, pork, and rice. The last three items formed the staple diet of the people of Hangzhou. In the streets were storytellers, acrobats, dancing, shadow-play, jugglers, puppets and musicians.

Marco Polo delighted in the city, and here are five more of his observations:

Source A
The most noble city, and the best that is in the world.

Source B
On the bank of this canal are constructed large stone buildings, in which all the merchants who come from India and elsewhere store their wares so that they may be near and handy to the market squares.

Source C

There are 10 principal market-places, not to speak of innumerable local ones. These are square, being one kilometre each way, and in each of these squares, for three days in the week, there is a gathering of 40–50,000 people, who come to market bringing everything that could be desired to sustain life.

Source D

If the guards come across some poor man by day, who is unable to work on account of illness, they take him to one of the hospitals, of which there are many. When he is cured he is compelled to practise some trade.

Source E

A voyage on the Lake offers more refreshment and delectation than any other experience on earth. There is an endless procession of barges thronged with pleasure seekers, for the people of the city think of nothing else, once they have done the work of their craft or trade, but to spend a part of the day with their womenfolk.

How important was trade?

A plan of Hangzhou. A local saying was:

- 'vegetables from the east ...' there was a vegetable market and vegetable gardens in the eastern suburbs
- 'Water from the west ...' drinking water came from the West Lake
- 'Wood from the south ...' wood came by boat, upriver from the interior
- 'Rice from the north ...' by canal from the plains; it was estimated that about 210–280,000 kilos of rice per day was consumed

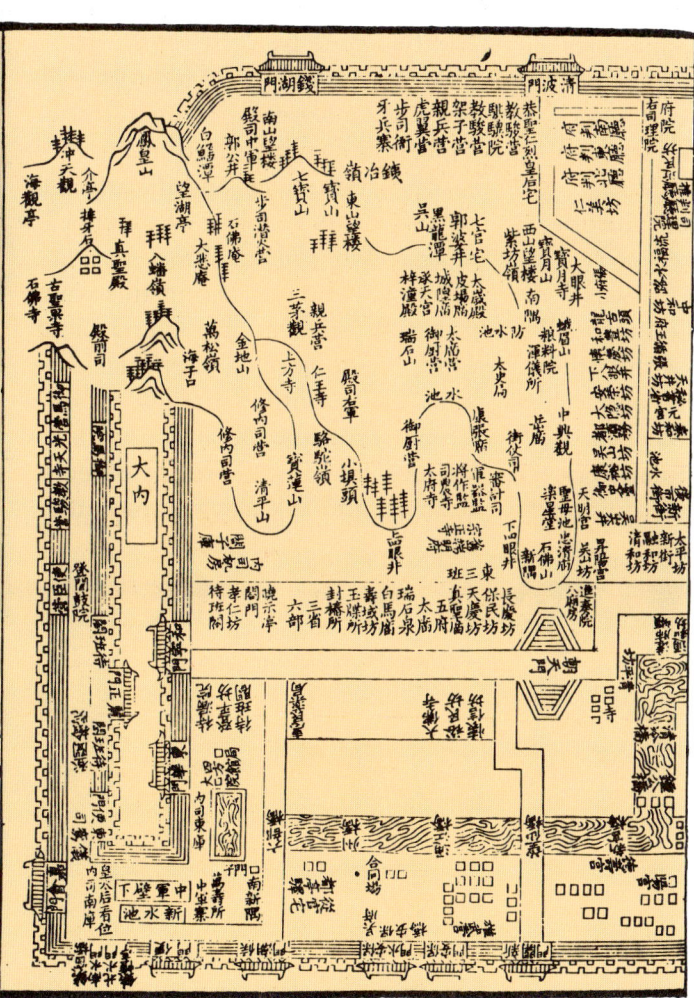
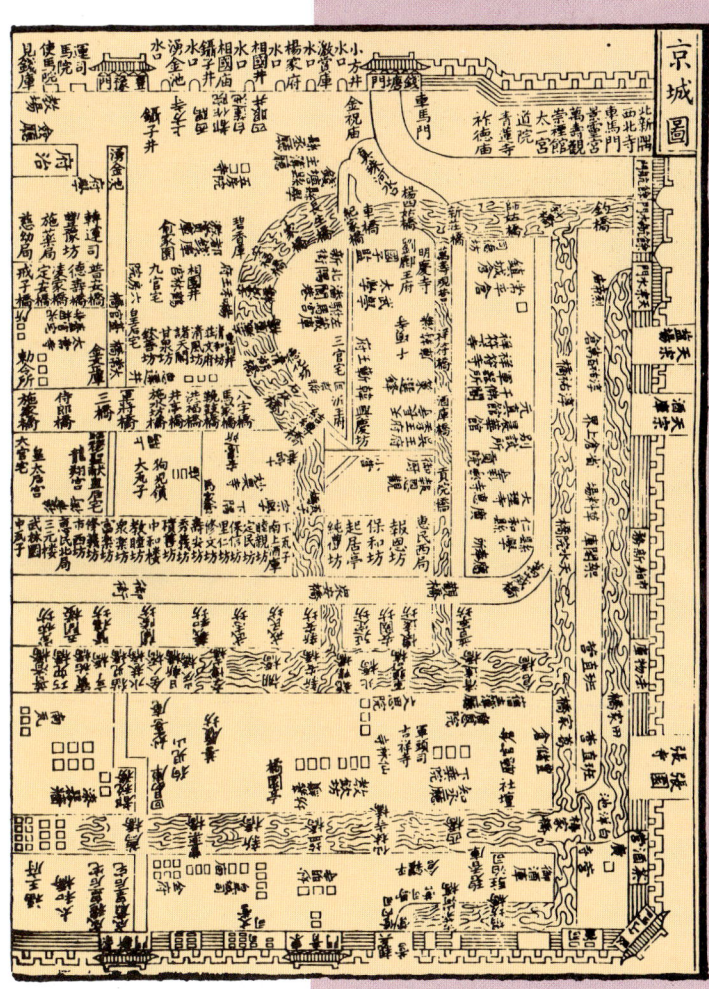

About two-thirds of the one million people who lived there did so within an area built in the seventh century, so dwellings grew upwards to house the increasing population. You can clearly see the many canals which crossed the city.

CHANGES: LIFE AND TRADE IN THE CITIES

1. What impressions do you obtain of Chang'an from the criticisms of 81 BC?
2. List the activities depicted in the Kaifeng scroll.
3. **a** Find out in your school library about a European city in the thirteenth century – like London or Paris.
   b Compare it with Hangzhou, and in two columns list the similarities and the differences.
   c What do you learn about China from this comparison?
4. What does this study of such organised city life, over a long period of time, contribute to your ideas on China as a civilisation?

Chapter six

六 Trade: Inwards and outwards

Now you can find out the origins of some of the goods that were traded in the cities, and the destinations of the Chinese goods that were exchanged for them.

Trade with Asia and Europe

China seemed cut off physically with oceans to the east, steppes and deserts to the north and north-west, and mountains and jungles to the west and the south. China could if necessary be mainly self-sufficient. The Chinese never had as much contact with other peoples as did, for example, the peoples of the Mediterranean. However, China had long-established overland caravan-routes to Persia (Iran), Egypt, Greece, Rome, and Europe, as well as contact with Asian countries on the way. This was how Marco Polo travelled into China, as did so many of the other curious travellers, traders, and foreign representatives. By sea to India was the other popular trade-route. In time this became quicker and more efficient. By the time of the Song (960–1279), Chinese ships sailed in the Indian Ocean and the seas of south-east Asia. Chinese coins and porcelain have been found throughout the Middle East. The use of the mariner's compass was important on these long journeys.

The Silk Road

The most famous overland trade-route was called the Silk Road, and it linked China with Central Asia and to Rome by connecting the Yellow River to the Mediterranean Sea with a series of caravan trade routes. It was first used in the second century BC and its original purpose was as a line of defence against the nomads. Trade developed quickly along this route into central Asia. Into China came gold, ivory, coral, amber, glass, woollen and other textiles. From China went furs, ceramics, iron, lacquer, cinnamon, bronze objects, rhubarb and silk in vast amounts.

A map showing the Silk Road and other trading routes. The Silk Road began to be used when a merchant-explorer Zhang Qian was sent by the Emperor Han Wudi to West Turkestan in 138 BC to make an alliance against some northern barbarians. He failed in his mission, and after adventures he returned with magnificent horses. As a result trade with the north-west flourished along the Silk Road. It was important for the next 1500 years.

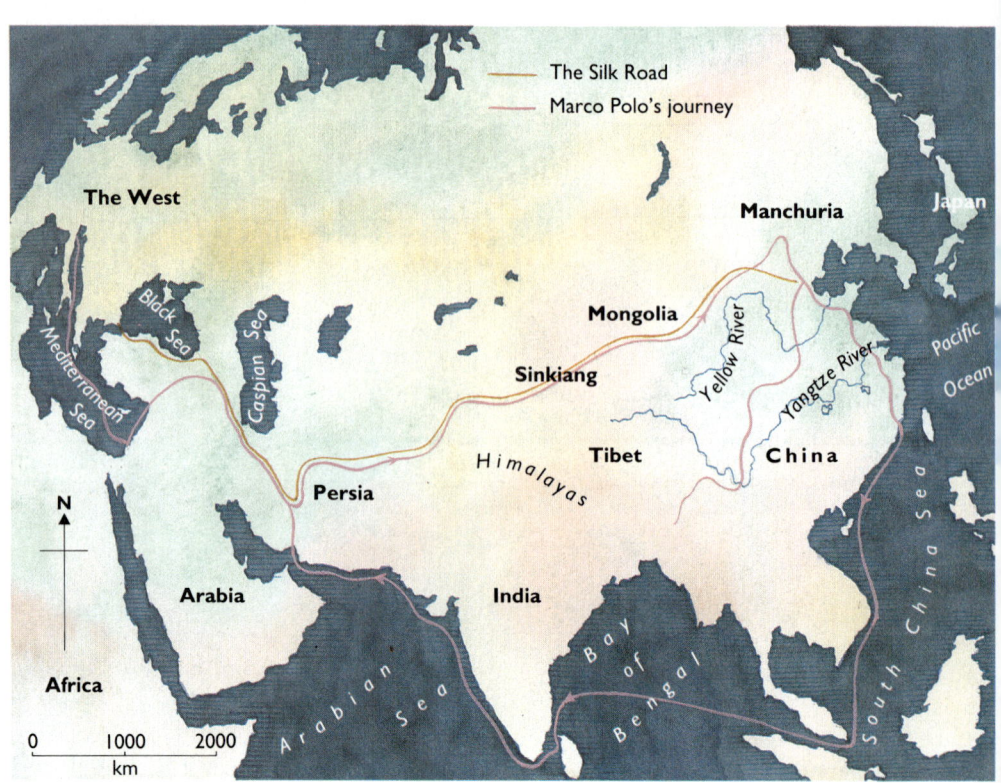

六 Trade and the four seas

Seagoing trade was mainly in Chinese hands but there were some foreign merchants – Muslims from Central Asia and India, Syrians, Persians (Iranians), Arabs and Jews. The goods that were imported into China were paid for by the exchange of Chinese commodities and by copper coins and metals like lead, tin, silver and gold. Chinese coins were so abundant in Japan that they were used as a local currency.

Chinese junks took silks, tea, brocades, porcelain, earthenware, gold, copper, silver, tin and lead, to:
- Japan
- the Hindu capital of Champa on the coast of Annam
- Malaya
- South India and Bengal
- the coast of Africa

In return came:
- ivory from India and Africa
- coral, agate, pearls, crystal, ebony, sandalwood, incense, cloves, and cardomon from other places

Junks were almost square in shape and had:
- 8–10 pairs of oars with 4 men to each oar in calm weather
- 2 stone anchors
- canvas or matting sails
- watertight compartments
- several dozen individual cabins
- 5–600 people and tons of food
- wood and water carried in a boat pulled behind

TRADE

1 Use the evidence on these pages to design a large poster about China and trade.
2 How does this information on trade contribute to what you already know about China?

Chapter six

✧ China and Europe: Views of each other

At the time of Christ there were two great Empires – Rome and China. The demand by the Romans for luxury goods grew, and they were soon buying silk in great quantities. However, the Romans remained ignorant of the origins and making of silk because trade was left in the hands of the Central Asian Silk Road merchants.

Because Rome and China had no direct contact only bits of information were passed between them. Neither was certain where the other country lay.

The Romans called the Chinese *Seres*, derived from *si*, the Chinese word for silk. This is how Pliny, a Roman writer from AD 23 to 79, described silk-making:

Source F
The Seres are famous for the fleecy product of their trees. This pale floss, which they find growing on the leaves, they wet with water, and then comb out, resulting in a double task for our women in first dressing the threads, and then again on weaving them into silk fabrics. So has toil to be multiplied; so have the ends of the earth to be traversed; and all for a Roman damsel to exhibit her charms in transparent gauze.

After the fall of the Roman Empire, Arab armies established a great Muslim Empire. This cut off Europe from China. Though trade continued, travel by Europeans into China did not take place until the thirteenth century. This did not worry the Chinese because they regarded China as better than any other country; they were content and confident that there was nothing to learn from other people. Nothing would change. China was the centre of the world. When European travellers did go to China in the thirteenth century, and took back information to Europe, it was as if there had been no previous contact.

One French traveller, Friar John, left on Easter Day 1245 and after one year of hardship arrived at Karakorum, the capital of the Mongol Empire. He did not visit China but met some Chinese whom he described.

A medieval map showing how Europeans saw the World.

DIFFERENT VIEWS: CHINA AND EUROPE

1. What do you learn from the map on page 47 about Chinese views of themselves, and of the World?
2. What do you learn from Sources F and G, and the map on page 46, about Europeans' views of themselves, and of the World?
3. Did the Chinese and the Europeans understand each other? Did they want to?
4. What does Friar John in Source G refer to about the Chinese? Why?
5. Read Marco Polo's comments about the Chinese again on pages 3 and 5. Were Friar John's comments about the Chinese the same as, or different from, those of Marco Polo?
6. Basing your answer on your knowledge of China, do you think these European travellers omit any key features of China? Explain your answer.
7. Was trade an important motive for these travellers, or were other reasons important?

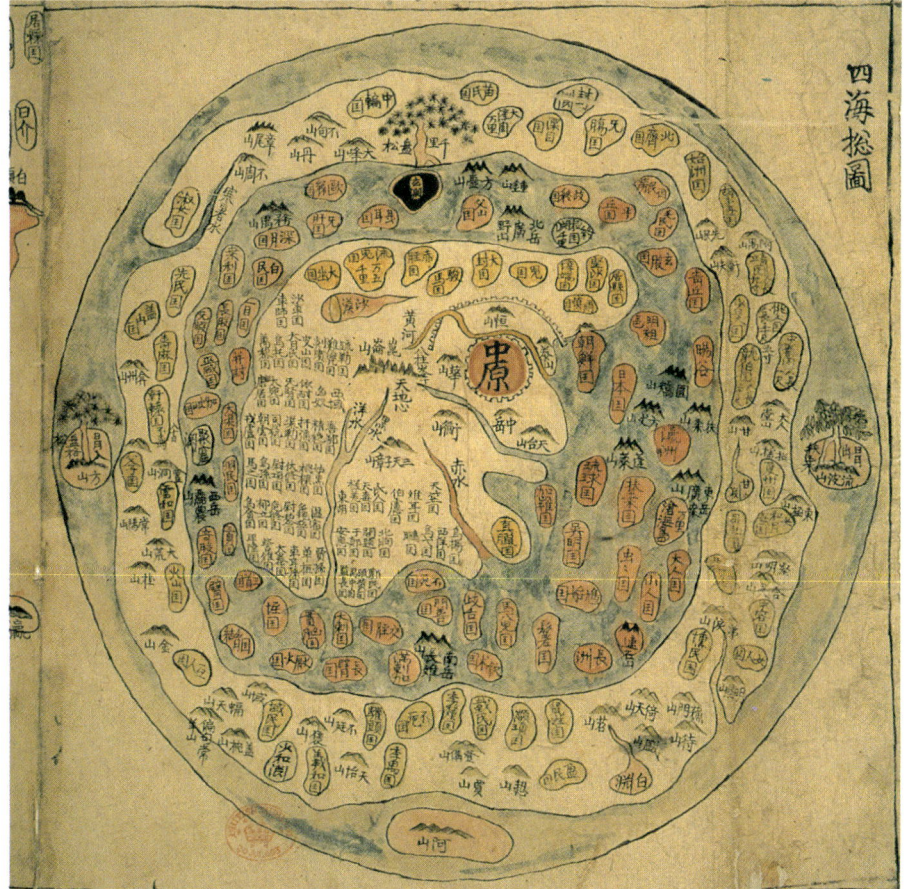

This eighteenth-century Korean map was drawn using ancient Chinese mapping ideas. China is the large land in the middle. You can also see the Great Wall marked on the map.

Source G
Now these Cathayans [Chinese] are heathen men, and have their own writing. It is said they have an Old and New Testament, and buildings which are used as churches, in which they pray at their own times, and they say they have also some saints of their own. They seem indeed to be kindly and polished enough folks. They have no beard, and have a considerable resemblance to the Mongols, but are not so broad in the face. They have a language of their own. Their betters as craftsmen in every art are not to be found in the whole world. Their country is very rich in wine, gold, silver, silk and in every kind of produce that man needs.

This is in contrast to the Mongols whose country he said was, 'more wretched than it is possible to describe.' The Khan turned down his offer of conversion, so Friar John returned to Europe, and died in 1252 probably feeling he had failed.

六 Conclusion

These early travellers to China were amazed at the very different world which they had seen, and feared that their fellow countrymen would not believe them. Friar John even ended his account with the names of witnesses of his journey, and stated that he had told 'the whole truth and nothing but the truth.' You believe him, don't you?

CONCLUDING YOUR INVESTIGATION OF CHINA AS A GREAT CIVILISATION

1 **a** The Chinese regarded themselves as superior. Why? List as many reasons as you can.
 b Do you think it was a reasonable judgement on the part of the Chinese?
 c Why were Europeans so amazed at what they saw and found in China, or what they heard about China?

2 Finally, think of all your ideas on China as a civilisation, including the negative features as well as the positive ones. In one paragraph, or several paragraphs, explain why China is regarded as a great civilisation from 221 BC to AD 1279. Add this for the last time to your wall display.

Index

Army 10–11, 18, 35

Books 9, 19
Bronze 4, 19, 23, 25
Buddha and Buddhism 15, 27–29

Calligraphy 5, 14, 21–22, 27
Chang'an (Xi'an) 8–10, 20, 26, 36, 41
Children 14, 32, 36
Cities (see also Chang'an, Hangzhou; Kaifeng) 41–43
Confucius and Confucianism 7, 14, 18–22, 27
Crafts 4–5, 10–11, 14, 19, 23–25, 29

Dao and Daoism 15, 39
Dragon 18
Dynasties 8, 19, 22
(see also Han, Qin, Tang and Song)

Education 19, 36
Emperor 9, 11, 14–15, 19, 32, 35
Entertainment 20, 26, 29, 39–42
Europe – see The West

Family 14, 32–33, 34–35
Farming 30–33
Festivals 39
Food 3, 30–33, 38, 41, 43
Friar John 5, 46–47

Great Wall 7, 9, 12–13
Government 9, 14, 21–22, 32
Gunpowder 4, 28

Han 8, 12, 18–19, 23–24, 32, 40
Hangzhou 3, 5, 8, 26, 38, 41, 42–43
Health 16, 17, 24
Heaven 14, 27
Homes 30, 31, 41

Inventions 4, 7, 28–29

Jade 24

Kaifeng 8, 42
Kites 28, 40
Kublai Khan 3, 47

Lacquer 23, 29

Magnetic Compass 28, 29
Maps 8, 12, 30, 44, 46–47
Marco Polo 3, 5, 7, 13, 22, 25, 35, 37, 44, 46
Medicine 16–17
Money 8, 9, 28

Officials 19, 20–21, 26, 32, 37

Paintings 27
Paper 4, 28
Peasants 12–13, 19, 26, 30–33, 35
Poetry 13, 26, 32, 34
Porcelain 25, 29
Printing 4, 15, 28

Qin Shihuangdi 8–10, 12–13

Rebellion 18, 32, 35
Religion 5, 15, 33, 47
Romans 6–7, 18, 46

Scholars 9, 36–37
Silk 7, 28, 31, 44, 46
Song 8, 25–26, 36, 42

Tang 4–5, 8, 14, 25–26, 38, 41
The West 7, 28–29, 44, 47

Women 3, 33–35
Writing 5, 8, 14, 19, 21

Xi'an (Chang'an) 8, 9, 10

Yangtze River 12, 25, 31
Yellow River 12, 25, 30

Acknowledgements

The publishers would like to thank the following for permission to reproduce illustrations:

Ancient Art & Architecture Collection pages 3, 10bl, 10br, 11br, 14tl, 15r, 16, 29; Bridgeman Art Library page 24t; British Library pages 46 (Add. MS. 15760, ff. 68v–69), 47 (Map Room c27.f.14); British Museum pages 4 (1935.10-27.1), 5 (1938.5-24.48), 23c (1974.2-26.44), 25t (1936.10-12.153), 26 (1936.10-9.038), 27l (1947.7-12.05), 27r (1910.2-12.0450); 32c (1973.7-26.171), 39b (1954.11-13.01); Cambridge University Press page 43; E.T. Archive pages 9, 14br, 38, 39t Werner Forman Archive page 42; Freer Gallery of Art, Washington DC page 32b; Magnum pages 10tl, 12, 31t (Hiroji Kubota), 31b (Zachmann); Magnum/Erich Lessing pages 6, 19t, 35; Nelson-Atkins Gallery of Art, Kansas City, Missouri page 15c; Panos Pictures pages 30t (Alain le Garsmeur), 30b (Trevor Page), 31b; Robert Harding pages 11tr, 19b, 23t, 24b, 25b; Science Photo Library/Paul Biddle & Tim Malyon page 17; Master & Fellows of Trinity College, Cambridge page 7 (MS r.17.1 f.263r); Wellcome Institute for the History of Medicine page 34; Zefa page 23b.

Cover photograph: British Museum (1974.2-26.44)

Illustrations: Ch'en-Ling and Martin Sanders